Political
Development
and
Democratic
Theory

Political Development and Democratic Theory

Rethinking Comparative Politics

Steven J. Hood

M.E.Sharpe

Armonk, New York
London, England

Library of Congress Cataloging-in-Publication Data

Hood, Steven J.
  Political development and democractic theory : rethinking comparative politics /
by Steven J. Hood.
    p. cm.
Includes bibliographical references and index.
    ISBN 0-7656-1466-9 (alk. paper); ISBN 0-7656-1467-7 (pbk. : alk. paper)
    1. Democracy. 2. Democratization. 3. Liberalism. 4. Comparative government.
    I. Title.

JC421 .H66 2004
321.8—dc22

2003025475

Printed in the United States of America

BM (c)   10   9   8   7   6   5   4   3   2   1
BM (p)   10   9   8   7   6   5   4   3   2   1

To Kristin, Rachel, Rebekah, and Brigham

Contents

Preface

Comparative scholarship on democracy in the last two decades or so probably has been more productive than at any other time. Comparativists have published numerous theories and case studies on democratization and problems of democracy in countries where democracy has been the norm for some time. There is no doubt that much of this scholarship has been significant. The specific knowledge acquired about the experiences of countries and regions with democracy is unsurpassed in terms of factual and procedural details. Knowledge of leaders, political parties, the linkages between the economy and politics, and understanding of institutional aspects of democracy has been greatly enlarged; but as with all periods that follow great advances in scholarship, we are left with perennial questions: Why do some countries seem to be unable to complete democratic transitions? Why does democracy emerge in some states only to fail to consolidate? Why, at a time when so many states are turning away from authoritarianism, is there a lack of enthusiasm for democracy in countries that have been democratic for a significant period of time?

This book attempts to address these issues in a way most comparativists will deem unconventional. While comparativists have studied the challenges of democratic transition, consolidation, and problems of mature democracies as separate problems, this study argues that the problems each regime faces—whether the regime is democratic or in the process of democratizing—are the same, differing only by degree. Although we should not and cannot abandon our current methodologies and theories about democracy, we need to recover thinking about democracy that has been lost along the way. Our understanding of democracy has become too focused on the procedural and mechanical aspects of democracy. This has kept us from being able to give fuller assessments of the quality of democratic experiences. We need to reconsider what democratic philosophers say democracy entails and look beyond some of the details

we focus on—elections, leaders, political bargaining, economic policies
—and instead look at what a democratic regime is supposed to entail.
This requires more than a redefinition of terms and concepts, it requires
us to consider what the ideals of democracy are and how well regimes
are able to approximate these ideals.

As we consider the usefulness and shortcomings of contemporary
comparative democratic theory in conjunction with democratic philosophy, we will be better able to capture the essence of democracy. It is the
essence of democratic life that is most often missing in comparative
studies because we have become technicians who identify procedures,
democratic tests, and qualifying features to justify our assessments of
democracy. Most of these assessments involve aspects of political participation and checks and balances on government power, but they focus
very little on specific aspects of liberal rights and democratic virtues.
Our limited view of democracy causes us to discover "new" ideas about
democracy, though most of these ideas have been around for a very long
time and have been the focus of philosophers who study democracy.

This book is a modest attempt to call upon comparativists to reconsider our assumptions about democracy. Democracy is more than elections, more than democratic compromises, and more than Alexis de
Tocqueville's work on democratic institutions. Modern democracies are
regimes that are highly complex and require scholars to consider most
of the questions philosophers who study democracy consider: What do
we mean by democracy? How should people living in democracies think
about democracy? What are the essential democratic virtues that every
regime should foster? Are there really significant differences in democratic regimes? What can Tocqueville, the American founders, and other
democratic thinkers teach us about democracy that will improve our
work? How useful are our comparative methodologies when it comes to
understanding democracy?

Several scholars have been a great help in reviewing earlier drafts of
this book. My colleagues at Ursinus College, Paul Stern and Rebecca
Evans, provided detailed and careful comments of each chapter and
helped me reconsider many of the ideas I present in the book. Karl Fields
of the University of Puget Sound and Eric Hyer of Brigham Young University read the manuscript as reviewers for M.E. Sharpe and offered
further comments and encouragement. To these four scholars I owe a
great deal for their time and concern for a project that is controversial
and yet, I hope, useful. Any shortcomings of the book are my own, and

not those of my colleagues. I am also grateful to Cathy Bogusky at Ursinus, who helped me with technical changes to the manuscript. She saved me an incredible amount of time. My wife, Mary, has always been encouraging of my work and a good sport in listening to my excitement and frustrations about this book project. Finally, I have had many wonderful students through the years who have had the courage and determination to wrestle with difficult ideas and champion democracy. Their enthusiasm and hope for democracy's future is inspiring and keeps teaching a dynamic and meaningful vocation.

Political Development and Democratic Theory

1

The Spirit of Democracy

Czech president Vaclav Havel is one of those rare human beings who can articulate a vision of democracy that is both practical and ethical. His words engender hope for a better world. He has struggled to keep democratic hope alive throughout his career as a playwright, dissident, and politician. While under the watchful eye of the Czechoslovakian communists, Havel called upon people everywhere to examine competing claims about how we should live our lives and learn to trust our consciences above all other appeals to authority. He admonished us to resist the "irrational momentum of anonymous, impersonal, and inhuman power—the power of ideologies, systems, apparat, bureaucracy, artificial languages, and political slogans." Havel's message then and now is that by virtue of being human, we are free. Using language that would be familiar to the American founding fathers, Havel teaches us that living as free individuals liberates the highest aspirations and dignities of which human beings are capable.

> We must not be ashamed that we are capable of love, friendship, solidarity, sympathy, and tolerance, but just the opposite: We must set these fundamental dimensions of our humanity free from their "private" exile and accept them as the only genuine starting point of meaningful human community. We must be guided by our own reason and serve the truth under all circumstances as our own essential experience.[1]

Havel's stirring defense of freedom, conscience, and morality is echoed in the courageous calls for democracy that we hear from every corner of the globe. The heroes of democracy share Havel's vision of human potential as they fight for and strive to preserve freedom. They are student voices heard in Beijing's Tiananmen Square calling for Chinese democracy. They are the lamentations of Las Madres de la Plaza de Mayo or "Mothers of the Disappeared" in Buenos Aires, who protest the torture, imprisonment, and death of their children at the hands of government thugs. Democracy is understood as a feeling, a unity of hope captured in the simple utterance of a shopkeeper in Mexico City following the first freely contested presidential election in Mexico. "The people finally showed that we are more powerful than any political party, even a dictatorship like the Partido Revolucionario Institucional [Institutional Revolutionary Party (PRI)]. Now we are in control."[2]

The fervor felt for democracy is more than a love for civil rights. Democracy embodies a faith that a more moral, prosperous, and dignified way of living exists than being ruled by others. Democracy represents liberty and responsibility, the pursuit of happiness, and civic duty. Many keep the promise of democracy alive. Courageous democrats continue to forge ahead in countries where democracy is still a distant hope, in countries trying to solidify democratic gains, and in established democracies where vigilance is needed to keep democratic hope vibrant. But while the promise of democracy remains alive, our scholarship on democracy has become moribund.

Comparative politics has done a good job of analyzing elite behavior and the importance of political bargaining, but we have failed to offer a comprehensive picture of the democratic promise. We have failed to capture the spirit of democracy. The reason for our failure is that we do not understand democratic philosophy. In fact, comparativists are largely ignorant of democratic philosophy and political philosophy in general. We teach our students what we know, which is primarily a few decades of social science methodology, but we are illiterate when it comes to knowing something about the great philosophies that examine democracy. We miss essential elements that explain deeper and more sophisticated reasons why countries democratize and why citizens in established democracies lose faith in their governments.

This book is about democratic development and the promise of democracy. An explosion of studies has surfaced in the last decade that analyze the processes of democratization. This book sorts out the major theories that scholars have developed to explain democratic development, offers some criticisms of these theories, and reintroduces a few timeless insights on democratization that have been overlooked by comparativists. Comparative politics has come to accept theory about democratization and democracy that is too narrow in its perspective and limited in its ability to fully explain the appeal and promise of democracy. This book calls for a comprehensive framework to study democratic development—one that takes into consideration the quality of democracy, including liberal rights and virtues. It offers a standard to judge the quality of democracy in any country. We need a framework that goes beyond our mechanical and technical explanations of democracy and instead looks at democracy as a comprehensive regime that improves people's lives better than an authoritarian regime. No attempt is made to introduce new theory here but instead to suggest that comparativists consider more fully the contributions thinkers like Alexis de Tocqueville have made in understanding modern democracy. This will help us better appreciate why so many countries have embraced democracy and why our attention to the democratic transition and consolidation processes has caused us to overlook a great deal of the substance of democracy.

A Democratic Consensus?

The twentieth century provides startling examples of human beings trying to establish the best regime. Ancient and modern philosophers have theorized about the best regime. During the nineteenth century, the democratic advances in America, France, and Britain provided powerful evidence that democracy, notwithstanding its flaws, benefited humankind in ways never before realized. Until recently, however, democracy was only practiced in a handful of countries. Alongside the development of democratic institutions in a few Western countries, industrialization, colonization, imperialism, impoverishment, and war demanded the attention of political leaders and social reformers everywhere. Unfortunately, many of these nondemocratic leaders and reformers blamed democratic countries for the problems nondemocratic countries experienced. Others admired democracy but believed that other kinds of regimes were better suited to the specific conditions of their countries. As former Singapore president Lee Kuan Yew suggests, the "Western liberalism" of the United States is admirable, but ultimately "certain basics about human nature do not change. . . . Westerners have abandoned an ethical basis for society, believing that all problems are solvable by good government, which we in the East never believed possible."[3] By the late 1980s, authoritarian regimes in most of their varieties faltered and began

5

to liberalize. The foreign policies of Western countries reflected a greater earnestness in supporting democratic reform, and comparativists took renewed interest in the study of democratization. One scholar, Francis Fukuyama, enthusiastically proclaimed an "end to history," an end to authoritarianism, and a permanent victory for democracy. Democracy, it seemed, was the realization of the final goal of the history of humankind, the successful outcome of a long developmental process.[4]

We will briefly look at the reasons why authoritarianism has been rejected in so many countries and what key influences have encouraged democratization. Next, we will turn to a discussion of why there is a rebirth of scholarship devoted to democratization by comparativists and explain why it has been difficult to reach a common understanding of democracy. Then we will sketch out what we mean when we speak of transition to democracy, democratic consolidation, and established democracy.

The Collapse of Authoritarianism

The most urgent goal of any authoritarian regime, whether it be based on a totalitarian, religious, economic, moral, or any other principle, is to stay in power. The tools used to stay in power may differ somewhat due to the particular principles the regime is attempting to uphold. A Marxist regime must mobilize all resources at its disposal in pursuit of accomplishing the goal of the revolution. If the regime fails to convince the people of the primacy of the revolution, the regime loses its reason for existing, and a political collapse may be imminent.[5] Nontotalitarian authoritarian regimes may point to economic dangers, moral imperatives, evil forces within the country, or aggressive neighbors as justifications for their monopolizing power. This kind of regime may determine what coercive instruments are needed to enforce the monopoly of political power.

There are many kinds of authoritarian regimes. Leaders in Iran, Saudi Arabia, and Egypt rely on various interpretations of Islam to maintain power. Others, like the Confucian countries of East Asia, may claim that certain cultural attributes are superior to the messiness, disorder, and license that they perceive to exist in democratic states and therefore legitimize their brand of authoritarianism. Many heads of state all over the globe point to the necessity of economic growth as a precondition to democratic development. Leaders in Cote d'Ivoire, Liberia, and Haiti speak to the necessity of using armed force due to internal and external security concerns. The presidents of Peru, Argentina, and Russia claim to be democratic, even though the transition to democracy has stalled.

Authoritarian regimes may or may not seek experts outside of government to help them. They may tolerate some levels of free speech or discourage political discourse everywhere except within exclusive government circles of power. They may be able to employ brilliant economic plans or have no idea how to encourage economic growth. They may seek racial harmony, or instigate racial conflict. They may genuinely love their country and care deeply for the welfare of the people living in their countries, or they may despise the people and care only about themselves. They may have many friends among democratic countries, or few friends. They may have been respected by the United States at one time for their benevolent treatment of people living in their countries, only to be subsequently criticized by Washington for failing to become fully democratic.

Authoritarian governments may be led by a sultan, a fascist dictator, a military junta, a communist party politburo, a Western-educated professional, scholar, or religious leader, or a group of leaders that constitute a ruling body. Some authoritarian leaders respect democratic institutions that have developed in the West and elsewhere. Some are even willing to admit that democracy is the goal to which their country aspires, even though little or no progress is made year after year in reaching that goal. The common feature in understanding authoritarianism is that most authoritarians do not trust the people or the regime's political opponents. Authoritarians believe that they, by themselves, are best able to run the government and administer policies on behalf of the country. They fear opposition and the threat of opposition. Authoritarian regimes are ever suspicious of political opponents and fear circumstances that could lead to their loss of power. They may speak of political rights, but they are careful not to elaborate a specific notion of rights in any detail for fear of setting in motion calls for liberalization and democracy.

Authoritarian regimes can be dangerous to themselves, the people they rule, and to neighboring countries. While some may enjoy political calm and economic development for several years or decades, unexpected circumstances may become the catalyst for the regime taking harsh measures against its people. The growth of a small opposition movement, criticism within government ranks, public outcry over the handling of a specific problem, or even the occurrence of a natural disaster will heighten tension within an authoritarian regime. Under these circumstances, nervous leaders begin to identify political enemies and issue threats. Tension builds and good will is destroyed. As groups and interests collide, these difficulties can result in calls for democratization, liberalization without democratization, attempts to increase repression, political coups, or intense political crises. People living in such countries may or may not support efforts to democratize and may even opt for rule by the existing regime, even though the leaders may be resented for their repressive ways, corruption, and extravagant lifestyles. Regime opponents may demand replacement of the regime without opting for democracy, but political bargaining and negotiations may lead to democracy without any grassroots support for democracy. Sometimes democracy does not even emerge as an option as calls for a just and moral, benevolent authoritarian regime are renewed.

But does a truly benevolent authoritarian regime exist—one where people are respected and enjoy equal treatment under the law? Where peace and prosperity are lasting? Where people have sufficient faith that the regime will not behave in an unfair manner? Leaders in some states, for example, make the claim that they live by the doctrines of Islam and therefore provide what is best for the people. However, scholars and religious leaders do not agree that this is the case. Most scholars believe that leaders of countries in the Islamic world use Islam as a tool to maintain exclusive political rule, rather than as a moral code to guide their lives, and they point out the contradictions between Islamic religious doctrine and political practice. [6]

From time to time philosophers have suggested that benevolent authoritarian regimes could develop that rival democracy in their capacity to administer justice and freedom. Yet, pending some unknown set of circumstances that would introduce such a political regime, most comparativists are united in their belief that democracy is the only form of government capable of providing adequate protection for people to function in a climate without fear. Political practices are based on such lofty ideals as justice, tolerance, equality, and freedom rather than threats, imprisonment, and death.

The Rise of Democracy

As disillusion and failure grow among despotic regimes in all their forms, key influences have helped bring about a reconsideration of democracy.

Democracy's advocates are found in every corner of the globe and represent a variety of interests. An overlapping network of international, regional, economic, and religious influences are united in their calls for democracy.

International Democratic Influences

Most international organizations encourage and operate by democratic procedure. These organizations provide valuable lessons to authoritarian leaders and very often carry the moral authority and representation of the world's most respected democracies. Organizations like the United Nations (UN) often carry considerable political power, making it impossible for states like the Soviet Union and China to decline membership. Membership in the UN requires member states to operate by democratic rules. The influence of foreign policies of democratic countries also has a significant impact in promoting democratic values worldwide. The UN, the European Union, and human rights organizations openly encourage democratic reform. They offer incentives of financial aid, technological assistance, and membership in their organizations for progress made in the areas of market reform, human rights, and democratic development. The United States and other countries have made greater efforts to link trade and other exchanges between themselves and nondemocratic countries on the basis of political reform. As authoritarian states become democratic, other authoritarian states find themselves increasingly isolated in the international community. This increases pressure on existing regimes to reform or risk driving their countries into economic ruin and political estrangement.

The steady increase in the number of democratic countries (from 69 in 1989 to 117 in 1999 by one organization's estimate) has set a new standard of governance.[7] The opportunities to maintain authoritarianism at home and still enjoy the support of the United States and other countries has diminished considerably. The United States no longer has an urgent need of making friends with whomever opposes communism. This has freed critics of authoritarianism in the United States and elsewhere to encourage authoritarian regimes to make democratic compromises. A simultaneous explosion has taken place in the number of nongovernmental organizations that watch and report on the human rights records of authoritarian regimes everywhere. Opposition leaders use these reports in their protests against oppressive regimes. Democratic governments and international organizations have come to rely on these reports in their deliberations relating to defense and trade agreements and other forms of development assistance. This has prompted authoritarian regimes to explain their treatment of prisoners and opposition leaders and to elaborate plans on how they are going to liberalize their regimes. In some cases governments have had to fashion policies that explain why they are going to proceed with their authoritarian ways. In spite of such resolve to maintain power, it is nevertheless significant that these governments no longer simply dismiss allegations of human rights abuse but, rather, feel they must justify their actions. Such a response indicates the growing impact that democratization and the human rights agenda is having on authoritarian regimes.

In a climate of increased democratization, significant pressure is placed on authoritarian leaders to avoid acting like pariahs. Democratic reforms are most likely the prerequisites that will allow countries to receive aid, trade, and security agreements, and democratic reforms are also the main way countries become esteemed members of the international community. Representatives of authoritarian governments are more likely to attend international meetings and listen to criticism of their harsh ways by representatives of established democracies and newly democratized countries than they were in the past. They realize the well-being of their countries in the international community is in part dependent on going along with the rules that are set by the world's democracies. Many leaders do not want the legacy of being the last dictators on the block— especially if their neighbors have democratized recently. They feel obligated to follow the route taken by other regimes that have made the successful transition to democracy. Military rulers hang up their uniforms and don business suits. They may go only a short distance in liberalizing their regimes or they may create only the barest trappings of democracy, but they recognize the necessity for reform.[8] Others liberalize the system without intending to democratize but find the pressures in maintaining power too great to hold back democratization. Authoritarians begin to consider how they will be treated in the history books and realize a positive legacy requires taking a lead in the democratization process. The international community will continue to be torn by competing interests and powers. Some of these encourage democracy while others discourage it, but recent history has shown that international influences, whether they be foreign policies, international rules, or peer pressure, have indeed played an increasingly positive role in the democratization process.

Economic Influences on Democracy

Some authoritarian governments have been very successful in promoting economic development. The authoritarian regime can muster its resources to promote specific industries it believes can facilitate domestic development and earn foreign currency through trade. It can fund the building of factories, refineries, and mineral extraction. It can marshal resources to transport raw materials and finished products. It can build port facilities to export products. Workers can be educated and trained, so they can find employment in the new economy. Unfortunately, authoritarian countries have not always proven to be successful in keeping economic growth going for the long haul, and some have proven unable to facilitate any kind of economic development.

Any government must face economic slowdowns and other financial crises. Economic woes have threatened and brought down democratic regimes, as well as authoritarian ones. However, established democracies are better equipped to weather economic storms than are established authoritarian regimes, thus they provide a model for authoritarians. Economic crises undermine the legitimacy of authoritarian regimes that rely solely upon economic success. Some authoritarian regimes try to buy time by inviting in outside experts to offer policy advice. These experts are often educated in the United States, or at least they are familiar with liberal economic theory, and they can suggest a number of liberalized policies to restart the economy. Whether they are economists or engineers, these better-educated experts realize the importance of economic cooperation between the private and government sectors to foster economic growth; they realize the importance of political freedom to entrepreneurial success and the building of a well-diversified economy. The advice of experts is a key reason why the former communist states of Eastern Europe are turning to democracy. Leaders see the promise and interconnected relationship of political and economic freedom. Authoritarians who resist calls for reform end up incurring the wrath not only of respected economic and industrial leaders outside the government, but also of reform-minded leaders who belong to the regime. The greatest hope for economic recovery, therefore, may include a democratic transition.

Sometimes economic success can lead to calls for democratization. The East Asian economic miracles played an important role in the political miracles that followed. In both Taiwan and South Korea the improvement in living standards and the growth of information sources led to the development of a large and powerful middle class. In time, a bourgeois spirit emerged that eased these countries toward democratic compromise. Leaders in both countries realized that the economic health of their nations required economic diversification, which could only come about as the political system became more democratic.[9] Residual economic inequalities in Latin America and other areas have limited and in some cases thwarted democratic reforms. In such cases, neither economic nor political promise seems bright. For many recently democratized countries, and in those countries where leaders are pondering a transition to democracy, the message seems increasingly clear. Authoritarian regimes are finding economic reforms and democratization more likely to correct economic disasters and expand economic possibilities.

Religious Influences and Democratization

Although more than three decades have passed since the Roman Catholic Church endorsed the political rights of its members in the Second Vatican Council, the impact on democracy has been substantial, especially in Southern and Eastern Europe and Latin America. Prior to Vatican II, the Catholic Church had been closely associated with authoritarian regimes in these regions, not because the church wanted to usurp the political rights of the people living there, but because it wanted to provide a way for people to earn their eternal reward. Authoritarian governments in Catholic countries were rarely criticized by Catholic leaders for abusing their citizens. Authoritarian rulers supported the church insofar as their tendency to stay out of church affairs, and in some cases, they even sought out the support of local church leaders. In some Catholic countries, the church and government signed agreements that defined the territory of the church and the state as distinct entities. The church was given privileges in education, social services, charity, and health care, and the state governed everything else. In some instances, governments were obligated to aid the church, and the church was expected to take sides in political debates.

However, church leaders were concerned about the intimate involvement of the church in state affairs and the perception that Catholics actively supported authoritarians, while Protestants supported liberals. They also worried about the persecution of non-Catholics in Catholic-dominant countries. American bishops complained that as Catholic influence grew in some countries, repressive measures were taken against Protestant minorities and followers of other religions. They called upon the church to proclaim unequivocally that it supported religious freedom and freedom of conscience on all matters related to religion and politics.[10] There was hope that the church would not only be a presence in these countries, but set an example for governments to follow in conducting civil affairs.

After lengthy debate, the "Declaration of Religious Freedom" was approved by the Second Vatican Council on December 7, 1965. It called for "immunity from external coercion as well as psychological freedom," in matters of religious preference. Government would clearly "transgress the limits set to its power, were it to presume to command or inhibit acts that are religious." It encouraged governments to establish people's rights because the "protection and promotion of the inviolable rights of man ranks among the essential duties of government."[11] It would take some time for the contents of the declaration to have the desired impact in Catholic-dominant countries ruled by authoritarian regimes. In some cases, the declaration helped encourage liberation theologians (religious leaders who call for political freedom in their religious teachings) and activist priests who openly rebelled against authoritarian governments. The real impact of Vatican II has been more recent, however. Separating the church from the state apparatus, in conjunction with other pressures for democratization, provided a strong base from which opponents of authoritarianism could operate.

Calls to liberalize Islam have not been as successful. Through the work of St. Thomas Aquinas, the Protestant reformers, and others, Christianity has been able to remove itself more fully from the state than has Islam. Freedom of thought has become a precondition to religious belief in Christianity in a way that many Muslims find offensive. To separate belief in God from its connectedness to the state is considered blasphemous to many in the Islamic world. Indeed, the calls for "Islamic democracy" stem from the work of fundamentalist intellectuals, who consider modern democratic institutions such as those found in the West a great threat to Islam. Critics point out that Islamic democracy is a relatively new development in Muslim scholarly discourse that does not acknowledge the openness of discussion practiced among traditional scholars of Islam (the *ulama*).[12] Proponents argue that Islamic countries need more than open scholarly dialogue, they need reformers who can reconcile Islam and democratic thought.[13] This conflict is familiar to those who advocated democracy in predominantly Catholic states prior to Vatican II, and it continues to constitute a major reason why democratization remains a remote possibility at present in most Islam-dominant countries. It is evident, however, based on the experiences of Catholics in authoritarian countries, that a religious criticism of authoritarianism helps to create conditions that favor democracy.

Comparative Politics and Democratic Development

From the previous discussion, it may appear as though it was inevitable that democracy would sweep the globe. This is certainly not the case. Even though the current trend of democratization has ushered in a new era of democratic acceptance, there are still many countries that remain authoritarian, and there are always countries that will fail to make democracy work and therefore fall back to their authoritarian ways. In addition, even the strongest democratic governments are not immune from democratic demise. The failure of scholars to fully appreciate democracy's unpredictable course nearly destroyed the subfield of comparative politics during the 1970s.[14] Thus, it is useful to look at how comparative scholars have viewed democratic development.

Comparative Politics' Schizophrenic Views of Democracy

As a distinct subfield, comparative politics emerged during and immediately following World War II. Prior to that time, most comparative studies were not really comparative. There were scholars who looked at governments other than their own, but most of these studies were attempts to classify and describe individual regimes rather than to compare the experiences of regime types. These studies were rudimentary and not very sophisticated. They primarily looked at constitutions, government structure, and other data to describe what a system did rather than to analyze a regime and assess its strengths and weaknesses. It is curious that comparative politics operated in such fashion given the grand analyses left to us by political philosophy.

In his *Politics*, Aristotle gave us a masterful analysis of regime types in considering matters of government structure, culture, economics, and political principle. He suggested that a regime is the political arrangement of authority. If the people have authority, the regime is democratic because the body of people rule. If the few rule for themselves or if a single person rules for him or herself, the regime is errant because these regimes do not consider the common good.[15] Charles de Secondat Montesquieu agreed with Aristotle's definition of a regime and argued that we need to also consider regime types on the basis of who benefits from the rule. His *Spirit of the Laws* details conditions that give rise to despotic, monarchical, and democratic regimes.[16] It is a powerful study that is still relevant today. In spite of these and other complete works from political philosophers, early comparativists in the twentieth century more or less assumed that democracy was the best regime possible and therefore failed to discuss the philosophy behind democracy. Overlooking the theory behind democracy lead to superficial analyses and generalities that lacked meaning.

Realizing that comparative politics as a discipline lacked theory, postwar comparativists relied on the methods of sociologists like Max Weber and Talcott Parsons to study systems.[17] But these methods were not much of an improvement from pre-war studies. Using ideal types (theoretical models of regimes) as benchmarks for comparisons, comparativists researched how the work of politics was accomplished in various countries. A problem with the research, however, was that the method used for studying politics reduced all political functions, regardless of regime type, into the same category. David Easton, for example, suggested that all regimes perform the same functions. These functions were influenced by the particular demands and supports of the political environment, and regime differentiation was determined by *how* the parts of the system performed their work. While all regimes had to make and enforce laws, develop economies, and educate people, the political environment determined which *parts* of the regime would be emphasized in performing these tasks. Unfortunately, Easton's work on regime analysis offered little assistance in determining the desirability of one regime over another, because it did not require the scholar to do much beyond classifying and identifying the efficient parts of a regime.[18]

Other comparativists like Gabriel Almond, Sidney Verba, and Lucian Pye suggested that comparativists needed to look at the defining role of culture.[19] They believed that the best way to study comparative politics was not by looking at what functions government performed but, rather, what cultural influences shaped political attitudes and decisionmaking. Having a clear bias toward democracy, these studies on civic culture sought to uncover the secrets underlying democratic success in established democracies so that authoritarian regimes could duplicate these conditions and become democratic. The civic culture studies were quite influential in launching efforts to understand political development, or how countries could become democratic. Aspects of the cultural approach are still widely accepted by comparativists today, even though this approach, and most methodologies that favored democracy, lost popular acceptance by the 1970s.[20]

The study of culture and politics convinced some scholars that culture was too important a determinant to single out cultural characteristics that could lead to democracy. Scholars like Pye suggested that much of political science's strength was due to the "acceptance of cultural relativism, to efforts at understanding the realities of actual political operations, and to a moratorium on debates about the ideal state of governments."[20] By this logic, political development need not be restricted to the acceptance of democracy as the only modern or developed form of government. Political development could include a number of things: prerequisites to economic and industrial development, abandonment of traditional ways of behavior, administrative effectiveness, social development, and democratic development. In defining political development in this manner, comparativists would consider other forms of government (other than democracy) as developed because they were accurate expressions of particular cultures. Cultures were different, and therefore the regimes they produced were relative to one another.[21] Studies of political culture minimized the importance of Almond and Verba's civic culture studies and instead introduced suspicion toward claims of cultural compatibility and democratic development in non-Western cultures. The acceptance of cultural relativism contributed greatly to the debate about the desirability of democracy within the subfield of comparative politics and helped fuel criticism of existing methodologies that favored democracy and specific democratic states.

While some scholars agreed that the role of culture was important in understanding political regimes, they also believed the state—the leading political organizations, both governmental and nongovernmental—had been overlooked by scholars who had overemphasized the role of culture and regime development. They suggested that comparativists needed to refocus on the state in order to understand the complex role of politics in democratic and authoritarian states and to see that states have the power to introduce change in a political culture. They argued this more dynamic way of understanding political regimes had been lost to reductionist attempts to understand politics by employing single-causal theories like culture studies.[22] Others criticized political culture studies for lacking theoretical strength. Rather than looking at how countries could become democratic, these scholars suggested we focus our efforts on why countries are developing into new kinds of authoritarian regimes. In particular, we should look at how capitalism destroyed the prospects for meaningful development and led to the establishment of regimes dominated by large and powerful bureaucracies. These bureaucratic-authoritarian studies encouraged us to look at states that focus on economic development at the expense of extending economic equality and rights.[23] They called upon us to consider how governments reacted to the demands of citizens who felt crushed by economic injustice. These "democratic" movements were seen as clear threats to authoritarian regimes. The 1970s also saw the rise of influential radical approaches to studying the politics of countries. Marxists and radical non-Marxists believed that regimes were in large measure economically determined. They called for changes in how wealthy countries interacted with nonwealthy countries. They suggested that the economic and political leaders of rich and poor countries had failed, and in some cases, had purposely avoided extending economic opportunities to people of all economic classes.[24] These studies criticized nonradical scholarship as biased examples of Western liberalism that overlooked the real problems poor countries faced. They claimed that many proponents of democracy excused the economic domination of poor countries in order to justify the accumulation of economic wealth in rich countries.[25]

While the radical approaches enjoyed much popularity during the 1970s and the early 1980s, other "mainstream" approaches persevered. These shared some of the concerns about democratic quality that democratic philosophers held. Samuel Huntington helped comparativists understand that authoritarianism could, in fact, lead to democracy as leaders attempt to bring order to societies that might otherwise be torn by violence, military coups, and other aspects of political instability. In attempting to bring about this order, authoritarian institutions sometimes change, clearing the way for liberalizing reforms.[26] Juan Linz and Alfred Stepan helped us understand that democratic failure in any given country could be temporary.[27] Other scholars suggested that comparativists initially had been too optimistic in our expectations for democratic development; but our understanding of the factors involved in democratic development were improving, and this knowledge could help us explain why countries were struggling with either authoritarianism or democracy.[28] Comparativists found themselves torn among three traditions: the cultural/behavioralists; the radical comparativists; and mainstream comparative politics.

Radical approaches to studying comparative politics and the class-based theories of politics lost much of their influence by the late 1980s. The primary reason for this was a major trend of democratization that took many scholars by surprise. Dubbed the third wave by Samuel Huntington, this trend toward democracy began with the democratization of Portugal, Spain, and Greece in the 1980s, continuing with democratic movements in Latin America, East Asia, Eastern Europe, and Africa.[29] The third wave of democratization has been so impressive that comparative politics, and political development in particular, has been revived. Democracy is once again the primary focus of comparative politics. Still, one should be concerned at how comparative politics has been overly influenced by popular trends in social science methodology. In summary:

1. Because of its preoccupation with domestic politics, early comparative studies emphasized the description of regimes rather than the analysis of regimes. This trend was exacerbated by Weberian ideal-type analysis that reduced all regimes to performing the same functions and aspiring to the same political ends regardless of regime type. By overlooking the inherent reasons different regimes exist, these early studies lacked explanatory power.

2. While culture studies of the 1950s and 1960s refocused comparative politics to the primacy of democracy, the embrace of behavioral methodologies moved comparative politics away from focusing on politics per se. Eventually culture was used to justify any kind of regime, regardless of its quality or promise, and many began to view democracy as a regime ultimately appropriate to only a handful of countries.

3. Radical approaches reflected mostly the dismay with liberal policies and democratic political thought. This was in part an outgrowth of the American experience in Vietnam, the lack of economic growth in Third World countries, the reversal of democracy and legacy of authoritarianism, and discouragement over the slow pace of democratization in the 1960s and 1970s.

4. Democracy once again became the focus of comparative politics, primarily because of the rejection of authoritarianism and the trend toward democratization that was apparent by the mid- to late 1980s.

It is evident from this brief sketch that comparative politics has failed to do what every good political scientist should do, namely, ask the question, "What is the best regime?" Doing so would have helped us focus on understanding the prospects for democracy. Political leaders could have turned to comparativists with greater confidence. Instead, they blazed the paths of democracy themselves, and we followed their lead; and while most comparativists are once again advocates of democracy, more attention is needed to address basic assumptions where uncertainties exist. Nowhere is this uncertainty greater than how comparativists have come to conceptualize democracy.

How Contemporary Comparativists View Democracy

Scholars have exerted great effort to theorize about how countries become democratic and what forces erase democratic gains.[30] While most comparative scholars assume democracy to be the best regime, they have adopted a rather limited working definition of democracy. For the most part, comparativists limit the definition of democracy to a set of processes. This is done for reasons of simplicity, and because detailed definitions of democracy are believed to bring in obscure or controversial preferences rather than basic realities of democracy. In their efforts to present a concise universal definition of democracy, however, comparativists have lost much of their ability to measure the quality of democracy—not only in general but also in comparing regimes—and this ability is essential to study the endurance of democracy.

Most comparativists rely on the definitions of democracy proposed by Joseph Schumpeter and Robert Dahl.[31] Schumpeter spent a good deal of time elaborating the key role that leaders play in democracies and the minimal role that people play. He is suspicious of the validity of concepts such as "the will of the people" because he believes the people support ideas that are given to them from their leaders. Therefore, he is quite critical of what he calls "the classical doctrine of democracy" because he believes it is idealistic and fails to address human nature properly and does not accurately portray the modern democratic process. For Schumpeter, how power is acquired and how political decisions are made are the key components toward understanding democracy. He argues that modern democracy is "that institutional arrangement for arriving at political decisions in which individuals acquire power to decide, by means of a competitive struggle for the people's vote."[32]

Dahl believes the characteristic that distinguishes democracy from other regimes is democracy's responsiveness to the preference of its citizens.[33] Like Schumpeter, Dahl also believes democracy is an approximate term and, therefore, believes that a good democracy demonstrates the quality of "being completely or almost completely responsive to all its citizens."[34] Rather than referring to this type of regime as a democracy, Dahl suggests we consider the term "polyarchy" instead, because modern democracies are not fully democratized, nor do they attempt to be. He believes polyarchy is a more accurate term because it can be used to define a regime that is "substantially popularized and liberalized, that is, highly inclusive and extensively open to public contestation."[35] Polyarchy reflects not pure democracy, but the inclusion of individuals, groups, and interests that compete in the political arena.[36] Hence, pluralism (the loosely rather than highly organized interests of groups, individuals, and public opinion) is a key component of democracy. Although some analysts have adopted the use of the term polyarchy, their use of the term democracy has an equivalent meaning to polyarchy.

While other scholars pay more attention to democratic theory in terms of rights, ownership, and the public realm, the emphasis is still clearly on democracy as a process of allocating power among office holders and making officials accountable for their actions.[37] Use of the term democracy by comparativists therefore makes the following assumptions:

1. Democracy, like all other forms of government, is a contest for political power. Other kinds of regimes seek to put power in the hands of the few, while democracy generally empowers the people, but specifically gives the power to make laws to elected representatives.
2. Elected representatives must compete for public office in fair and open elections and must be held accountable for their actions.
3. The most effective check on the abuse of power is the ballot box and the free distribution of and access to information.

Comparativists give an overwhelming amount of attention to contested elections as an indicator of democracy. Transitions to democracy are said to be complete when the first fully democratic election is held, and democracies are said to be consolidated when people accept the rules of democracy—which implicitly refers to the system of electing public officials and holding them responsible for their actions. No doubt, elections are vitally important. They are, after all, the most obvious indication that political power is not the exclusive domain of a single person, group, or class of people. But elections are simply one aspect of democracy, and the analysis of elections does not adequately address issues related to regime quality. Some countries have incredibly high voter turnout for elections, especially initial democratic elections. Other countries may have poor voter turnout, but democratic promise and the overall quality of democratic life remain high. In addition, the focus on elections does not emphasize fully enough the other rights and obligations associated with democracy, including the role that virtue plays in democracies—as mentioned at the beginning of this chapter, and as will be discussed in depth under the heading "Democratic Virtues." How, then, is it that elections became the determining element in defining democracy for comparativists?

Comparativists have not read political philosophy closely enough. Schmupeter's declaration that leaders play the decisive role in formulating the will of the people is not a new one. Similarly, Dahl's suggestion that the role of the individual in democracy competes with groups and common and competing interests is as old as democratic theory itself. The understanding of democracy as a polyarchy, in other words, has existed since the first formal theories of democracy appeared. A close reading of Greek political·thought reveals the important role that leaders play in instilling the ideas and principles that people should embrace for democracy to prevail. Classical thinkers understood the promise and danger of influential leaders, groups, and ideologies competing for influence in a democratic regime. In fact, classical treatments of democracy are far more suspicious of democratic idealism than either Schumpeter or Dahl appreciates[38] The works of modern democratic thinkers like John Locke, Montesquieu, Alexis de Tocqueville, and the American founding fathers reveal how we can address the weaknesses of democratic regimes with which ancient philosophers (and contemporary comparativists) were concerned. Comparativists focused on electoral processes at the expense of principles that are essential to democracy. Let us now turn to a discussion of what these principles are and how a better understanding of democracy is needed for comparativists to be able to shed light on the process of democratization in assessing the quality of specific democratic regimes.

A Fuller Understanding of Democracy

Modern democracy is built upon two components—rights and virtues. Both of these components belong to the tradition of liberalism associated with the work of Locke, Montesquieu, and the American founding fathers. While rights are considered to be more instinctual and something all human beings possess by nature, virtues are taught through liberal education and religion, as well as in the home.

Rights

The concept of rights is difficult to grasp, even in societies that formally recognize rights. It has become common for citizens living in democratic regimes to think of their rights as more important than virtues for a number of reasons. Virtues cannot be enforced by law, and citizens in democratic regimes tend to draw a definite line between what is legal and what is not. Also, the relative strength of virtues differs from one person to the next, whereas there tends to be broader agreement on the content and purpose of rights. For this reason, rights are less controversial to us as citizens than are virtues.

Our understanding of rights can be traced to the work of philosophers like Locke and Montesquieu. Locke saw individuals as "free agents" with inherent rights, based on the premise that all persons are ultimately equal in power, freedom, and in their desire for self-preservation.[39] He agreed with Thomas Jefferson's belief that human beings are created equal and are endowed with the particular rights of life, liberty, and the pursuit of happiness.[40] These individual rights correspond to the view of human nature that we are self-interested and will act accordingly. The acceptance of individual rights is a real challenge to political authority because it assumes that no single person or group of persons can, by nature, rule over others. Within the rubric of modern liberal democracy, the acknowledgement of individual rights was a prerequisite to establishing a regime with political rights. Political rights allow us to rule ourselves by selecting representatives to govern us as we would have them govern. Elected representatives are checked in their power by different branches of government, namely the legislative, judicial, and executive divisions of government, and by the creation of governments to represent the interests of people locally.[41] While all of these checks are intended to keep government leaders from usurping power, the different divisions and divided powers of government also guard against the rights of individuals or minorities from being abused. Political rights protect our desires to voice our political opinions, to assemble when we want, and to protest against undesirable government intervention in our lives.[42] The minimal requirements of the modern democratic regime, therefore, rest on the establishment of political rights, which are based on several key assumptions:

1. Human beings are free agents. They are not ultimately bound by custom, ancestral tradition, or other claims of moral or political superiority.
2. Human beings are free to challenge political authority. They have a right to scrutinize all moral, ethical, and political claims made by political leaders and determine the validity of such claims. They are free to consider all matters of public policy without fear of retribution, and government has been organized in a way to ensure this liberty.
3. Rights of equality, liberty, justice, and suffrage are based on a certain conception of human nature. In light of this understanding, the modern democratic regime is viewed as the best regime because it gives people a greater chance to pursue their interests than any other form of government.

Democratic Virtues

The French philosophers Montesquieu and Tocqueville and the American founding fathers accepted the liberal notion of rights as introduced by Locke. There was a prominent fear, however, that founding a republic only on rights would not have desirable results. Tocqueville believed virtue, particularly the Christian notion of virtue, offered much to offset the potential abuse of rights in the young American republic. He hoped America would connect Christian virtues and rights and hold the two as inseparable. Montesquieu believed that living in a republic tempered by virtues would make people behave better. Montesquieu, Tocqueville, and many of the American founding fathers feared that relying solely on rights as the basis for a democratic society would fail to adequately curb zealous self-interest, and they believed that Christian virtues would help people to develop strong morals, or habits of the heart, with which to govern their lives.

In many respects, these virtues complement the rights of Locke's liberalism. Compromise, fair play, and tolerance underscore the assumed rights of equality, justice, and the duties that these rights imply.

Montesquieu hoped that people living in republics would practice moderation and frugality and that they would maintain their sense of Christian shame, morals, and spirit of self-sacrifice.[43] Jefferson and other political thinkers believed it was vitally important to teach virtues in both religious and secular settings in order to keep society from becoming too reliant on rights.[44] Similarly, contemporary theorists suggest the virtues that should be taught include courage, obedience to the law, and loyalty to the democratic principles. Individuality must be developed in a way that encourages self-restraint, self-transcendence, and a firm belief that some ways of living are better than others.

Leaders in democratic societies must be willing to make difficult choices and must find common purposes to which society can aspire. They must be generous and prudent and possess noble ambition, pride, a sense of justice, and intelligence.[45] These virtues cannot be guaranteed in a democratic society, nor is the willful violation of these virtues necessarily a violation of rights.

In his observations of the young American republic, Tocqueville expressed his amazement at the citizens' level of self-governance. People had learned, through democratic practice and by their morals, to govern themselves through a wide variety of public institutions that were neither government-sponsored, nor familial. Reading groups, garden clubs, communal associations, scholarly associations, and even church groups had incorporated democratic principles and virtues to govern their behavior. Instead of finding a republic serving selfish interests, Tocqueville observed a civil society, where Americans' habits of the heart were connected to rights and formed adequate parameters for governing.[46] It is the creation of a civil society, or that level of governance that lies between the individual and the state, where democratic citizens set up their affairs and protect their interests that are separate from the state.[47] While some of these concerns have been rediscovered by comparativists, we have not come far enough.[48] The real measure of democratic success comes not by looking simply at the phenomena of democratic elections, but at the people's abilities to self-govern in a disciplined manner when drawing from virtuous principles. By using elections as barometers of democratic success, comparativists consider only one aspect of democracy and consequently often miss important clues in understanding the whole spectrum of democracy.

Some principles that enhance the prospects for, and maintenance of, democracy therefore include:

1. accepted standards of right and wrong based on individual accountability, and an acknowledgement that an individual's personal behavior has a direct influence on the well-being and happiness of others;
2. a sense of moderation, tolerance, fair play, courage, and frugality —which bring civility to public and private life; and
3. leaders who esteem high standards of virtue and believe that their words and actions provide a moral example for others to follow.

Comparativists can give a much richer interpretation of the process of democratization and better evaluate the quality of democracies in general by paying close attention to democracy as just described. Using a more philosophically based definition of democracy gives comparativists more explanatory and normative power and moves comparative politics beyond the tendency to classify and describe regimes.

The Phases of Democratization

Comparative theorists generally recognize three phases of democratization. Our concerns about how we view democracy and our assessment of the quality of particular democracies are completed within the context of these phases. In the actual process of democratization, few countries will democratize in an orderly course from one phase to the next. The processes of transition and consolidation sometimes occur simultaneously. Although there is a chapter devoted to each phase in detail, it is necessary to offer a broad definition of each phase now so a frame of reference is established.

Transitions

Scholars refer to a transition as the "interval between one political regime and another," even if the authoritarian regime in power is replaced by another authoritarian regime.[49] Some point out that transitions are unpredictable and many times fail to bring about a democratic compromise. Others suggest a true transition begins with the breakdown of an authoritarian regime and ends with the establishment of a democratic regime, characterized by free elections.[50] No doubt, authoritarian regimes can be in flux or completely unstable, but a transition must imply a transition

25

from one kind of regime to another, in this case a democratic transition. The best definition of transition, therefore, relies heavily on political circumstances that result in a transition from authoritarianism to democracy. Because a transition implies the completion of a process, a transition is only a transition when agreement is reached to end authoritarianism by the creation of institutions that allow for free elections.[51]

Consolidation

Just as scholars disagree about their conceptualization of a transition, they also disagree about democratic consolidation.[52] Some scholars suggest there is no such thing as consolidation, that democratic stability is based more upon economic development than any broad-based consensus on democratic institutions.[53] One scholar, Guillermo O'Donnell, suggests it is the effective functioning of a democratic regime.[54] Another, Andreas Schedler, suggests consolidation is institution building—in particular, the construction of all organizations necessary to move a regime beyond mere elections toward liberal democracy.[55] Most scholars who agree that consolidation is a real phenomenon also agree that it has a great deal to do with attitudes and democratic stability. Hence, Linz and Stepan provide the definition of consolidation that probably has the widest acceptance. They suggest that a democracy is consolidated when the realization occurs that it is "the only game in town"—meaning that a democratic regime is consolidated if no significant actors, national or international, attempt to replace it; if a substantial majority of public opinion believes that democracy is the best way to govern society; and if governmental and nongovernmental forces agree to solve conflicts as outlined by the rules of the democratic process.[56] This conceptualization of a consolidated democracy is useful and will be compared to the formulation of democracy described in the preceding discussion.

Established Democracy

Comparativists are once again researching and writing about the types of problems that established democracies face. Many comparativists are primarily concerned with the transition and consolidation phases of democracy because most countries of the Third Wave are wrestling with these phases. Some scholars do not refer to states where democracy persists as being established, but rather, as being advanced or mature democracies.

Perhaps an established democracy can be characterized by the existence of a strong notion of rights, democratic virtues, and confidence that democracy has an enduring quality not found in other regimes.

While comparativists today are doing much more theoretical work on established democracies, political philosophers have studied the enduring qualities of democracy and the problems of rights and virtues in these regimes for centuries. Thus, we will turn to the work of both modern and contemporary political philosophers to broaden our understanding of established democracies.

Our conceptualization of democracy strives to move us beyond short definitions, and it is hoped that within the context of each chapter, the reader will come away with a richer and more theoretically satisfying appreciation of what the concepts of transition, consolidation, and established democracy entail. Chapter 2 begins with an analysis of the strengths and weaknesses of contemporary studies of democratic transitions, and Chapter 3 assesses contemporary scholarship on consolidation. Chapters 4 and 5 are more philosophical in their approach, considering how democratic philosophy can help us produce richer and more accurate studies of democratization and democracy.

2

The Transition from Authoritarianism to Democracy

Comparativists have been engaged in a valiant attempt to understand and explain the transition from authoritarianism to democracy for several decades. It is a noble venture that has been of interest to political philosophers since antiquity. This chapter considers the attempts to explain democratic transitions, especially from the 1950s forward; the popular views of how democracy evolves; scholarly enthusiasm for, and discouragement with, democratization theory during the 1950s, 1960s, and 1970s; and the emergence of a mainstream approach to development studies that gained strength with the third wave of democratization. The chapter concludes by suggesting that much more can be done to explain transitions if the concerns of democratic political philosophy are considered more carefully. This will help us to understand the complexity of democratic transitions and to appreciate the attractiveness, promise, and superiority of democracy over authoritarianism.

The Popular View of How Democracy Evolves

The American understanding of democratic development can be traced to our romantic views of the American Revolution. "The people" are commonly referred to as the heroes of democracy because they fought a war of independence and established a government based on "life, liberty, and the pursuit of happiness." While this understanding is based on general truths, the historical details of the American Revolution, at best, are buried under a pile of partially accurate perceptions; the other truly great aspects of how the American republic was crafted are often overlooked. Indeed, many first-time students of political science, and even a few seasoned experts, hold an idealized view of how democracy defeats authoritarianism. Generally, this perception contains the following (false) assumptions:

1. In any given authoritarian country, the people are poor, honest, and oppressed. They completely understand principles like justice, equality, and liberty, as well as their political rights.
2. The government is headed by evil leaders who become wealthy from the taxes they collect from the people. These leaders imprison and execute people at will. They like to oppress people and spend considerable amounts of time trying to find new ways to get richer while increasing their repressive ways.
3. The people, on the other hand, can be satisfied only when popular rule is established through the creation of a democratic state. At some point, they will spontaneously rise up and overthrow the government.
4. Then, as soon as the rebellion begins, victory turns the rebels into peace-loving citizens. They turn their swords into plowshares and happily follow the rules of the new democratic regime.
5. Poverty ends, and the oppressors of the previous regime are tried in court and pay a bitter price for the pain they inflicted on the people. Justice prevails.

This scenario may seem absurd, but it is a drama that is retold time and again in the literature we read as children and adults, in the movies we watch, and in the abbreviated analyses we receive on our evening television news programs. Not only does our consumption of superficial, idealized accounts of political events convince us of the logic of this scenario, but also the truth contained in the scenario reinforces the popular view we hold of authoritarianism and democracy.

Post–World War II history provides dramatic examples of good and evil in the world. The Western democracies had little time to celebrate their victory over fascism before the communist regimes of Eastern Europe suppressed any hope of democracy for countries under the direct influence of the Soviet Union. The East German regime built a wall to keep its own people from escaping to freedom in West Germany. Almost simultaneously, infant democratic movements in Latin America and Asia were replaced by military governments, or civilian governments with no interest in opening their systems to democratic contestation. While America celebrated its bicentennial as an independent democratic state, the murderous Khmer Rouge regime of Cambodia was poised to begin its campaign to herd people into the countryside like livestock, where they became victims of a horrible social experiment that led to the destruction of Cambodian society. Thus, although most people living in the democratic countries of the world did not have a sophisticated understanding of the ambitious theories behind the communist revolutions in Europe and Asia or the reasons why democracy failed in Latin America, they did know that good regimes were democratic and bad regimes were authoritarian.

If the popular view of political development were completely true, the task of building a democratic regime would not be very arduous, and our federal government's foreign policies toward authoritarian countries would radically change. Based on the logic that all people living in authoritarian countries are convinced of the inherent goodness of democracy, the United States could plan coups d'etat and send in the Marine Corps at the slightest hint of popular support for overthrowing a regime. Popular uprisings would be successful in establishing democracy. Democratic states could educate citizens of nondemocratic states about the promise of democracy and receive immediate support and success. Before long, only democracies would exist in the world. The prospects for democracy would seem even rosier than they do now, and we would come closer to realizing sustained peace throughout the world.[1]

But we realize that this scenario is in part false because we understand authoritarian regimes enough to know that the factors supporting authoritarianism are complex, making prediction difficult. The realities of authoritarianism follow:

1. Not all people living in authoritarian countries are poor, honest, and oppressed. Many levels of economic well-being, political repression, and public and individual virtue exist in authoritarian states.

2. In most cases, people living in authoritarian states do not have a clear understanding of such democratic principles as justice, equality, and rights. In fact, they may hold a view of each of these principles that is antithetical to democracy. In some countries that have made the transition to democracy, the people were far more suspect of democracy than were the authoritarian leaders who willingly gave up power to complete the democratic transition. Scholarship on this subject suggests ideals such as justice and equality, as well as the appreciation of democratic rights, often are developed after democracy is established.[2]

3. As a general rule, popular revolutions do not defeat authoritarian

regimes. Popular revolts rarely are organized around a central vision of democracy, and they do not provide a suitable environment for political discussion between the opposition and those running the government. In many cases popular revolts diminish democratic hopes and result in harsher political repression.

4. Not all authoritarian leaders are viewed as evil. Some enjoy widespread support of the people, even though they may be suspected of doing, or even expected to do, things the people may find morally reprehensible. At the same time, some authoritarian leaders are perceived as highly moral and, in fact, use moral appeals to fight against the establishment of democracy.

5. Not every authoritarian regime executes dissidents, and some rarely imprison members of the opposition. Exclusive political control can be maintained without resorting to execution, torture, or imprisonment.

6. Deposed authoritarian rulers may not spend a single day in court for crimes committed under their watch. In some regards, it actually may be undesirable to hold such trials because the threat of prosecution may convince authoritarians of the need to postpone or cancel the transition to democracy.

7. The establishment of democracy does not guarantee economic success. Scholars are beginning to offer some connections between democratic development and economic development, but no direct causal relationship between the establishment of democracy and the emergence of a mature, highly diversified economy can be guaranteed.

8. The establishment of a democracy does not guarantee long-term democratic success. Some democracies collapse before any meaningful policies can emerge. Other countries have regimes that flounder back and forth between authoritarianism and democracy.

In some respects, scholars have made erroneous assumptions of their own in regard to the process of democratization. In the late 1950s and early 1960s, scholars understood the unpredictability of democratization, though their theories—which are listed below—still reflected much of the optimism and romanticism of democratization that is commonly held among the average proponent of democracy:

1. Mass support for democracy is necessary to make democracy take root. People need to be educated about the logic of democracy; then they will embrace democracy and make it work.

2. Indeed, democracy creates its own logic and staying power. Once

democracy gets a strong foothold, people become proponents of democracy for the long haul.

3. Economic modernization is a necessary requisite to democracy. Once modernization takes place, a middle class is established and democracy becomes the logical course to follow.

4. Remnants of the former regime must be rooted out. They must be placed on trial so that democratic citizens can feel a sense of justice.

Once again, if the problems were this straightforward, crafting democracies would be easier than is actually the case. The U.S. government once again could spend its time subverting authoritarianism by teaching citizens of authoritarian regimes about rights and why democracy is a better way. If, in fact, democracy creates its own logic, we could use our military to overthrow harsh regimes and establish democratic ones, and the logic of democracy would take over and solidify democratic gains. Wealthy democracies could flood authoritarian regimes with money in order to develop these countries economically, which would result in a strong middle class that would allow for democracy to emerge.

But our scholarship on democracy proved much too optimistic and in some cases simply wrong. The realities of democracy follow:

1. Mass support is not necessarily needed to establish a democratic state. In fact, mass support for democracy may not emerge until the consolidation phase of democracy rather than in the transition phase.

2. Educating citizens about democracy takes a long time. It took Americans decades to begin to understand the full potential of democracy. There are formal and nonformal processes for learning about democracy, and contemporary research suggests democratic education is transgenerational.

3. Democracy does not necessarily create its own logic. Sometimes logic suggests other regimes are more efficient and less corrupt than infant democracies.

4. Economic modernization is not a magic formula that creates democracies. Most scholars find economic development very helpful to democracy—especially if democratic proponents lend a hand in launching successful economic policies—but econom-

ics itself does not explain sufficiently why democratic transitions occur. *In fact, s*ome countries that adopt democracy are economically backward.

So what do we know about how transitions to democracy begin and why some transitions are successful while others are not? One might think that political science has learned little or nothing about democratic transitions. The truth is we know a great deal more about transitions today than we knew several decades ago. We have made progress in our attempts to understand democracy. Although we cannot predict with great certainty which countries will be successful in making the transition from authoritarianism to democracy, we do understand what factors improve the likelihood of a democratic transition and what factors work against democratic transitions.

Comparativists' Early Theories About Democratic Transitions

In the 1950s and 1960s, comparativists relied relatively little on political philosophy to understand democracy. They believed political philosophy addressed questions about the relative worth of democracy without really looking at how democracy emerged, flourished, or failed under modern conditions. Comparative politics, and indeed political science in general, accepted the methodology of modern social science based on the positivistic assumptions of Max Weber and others. Weber believed that modern social systems were the product of a rational world. As a country became more capitalist, there would be a corresponding rational development of government organs, in particular, the bureaucracy. Traditional political authority would give way to rational authority. Rational systems, based on specialization of interests and legal structures, were the most developed. Weber believed that the catalyst for, and development and maintenance of, rational political authority was capitalism.[3] From Weber and others, comparativists came to believe that capitalism, institutions, political attitudes, and cultural attributes could be studied in an objectified way, much the same as natural science looks at the process of cell division under a microscope. They believed that social science methods gave us power to understand human phenomena in ways not possible with traditional political philosophy because political philosophy too often constructed theoretical categories that did not address the real conditions of political regimes in the twentieth century.[4] Social science allowed us, through a combination of methodologies, to attempt to measure actual human attributes, thus predicting with greater accuracy than ever before what was needed to improve the human condition. Nothing demonstrated the excitement of social science more in this regard than the development of modernization theory and political culture theory.

Modernization Theory

Buoyed up by the economic development that occurred after World War II, modernization theorists tended to view economics and modernization as a cause/effect relationship. Like Marxists, modernization theorists believed that social change was linked closely to economics. Economic forces determined if a society would remain traditional or become modern. They believed that economic development would lead, not to the withering away of the state as proposed by Marxists, but instead to the creation of conditions favorable to democracy. Sometimes dubbed "linear development" because of the cause/effect relationship of economics to democracy, modernization theorists pointed to the correlation they saw between modernization theory and the creation of a middle class to whom political philosophers had pointed. Because established democracies were wealthy countries, modernization theorists directed attention to what they saw as a connection of wealth to democracy. Economic wealth was viewed as people's primary concern, after which all other factors, political and social, would find their place.

The appeal of modernization theory is readily apparent to anybody who pays attention to news reporting. Prominent journalists and scholars have attributed the end of the cold war as the victory of capitalism over the command economies of communism. This simplistic explanation would have been commonplace among early proponents of modernization theory. Daniel Lerner believed traditional societies were being transformed into modern societies as rural populations found their way to urban centers. In cities people developed skills and resources necessary in building a modern society. As the economy grew and as the population participated in this development, literacy skills improved drastically, and the influence of the media grew rapidly. The interaction of literate citizens and the growing importance of the media would lead to popular involvement in society at a level previously unrealized. The ultimate result would be increased political participation, eventually leading to democracy.[5]

While Lerner's thesis lacked important detail and explanatory power as far as democratization was concerned, his work seemed common sensical and contributed to a growing scholarly trend that explained democratization as a product of the process of economic modernization. In a way, Lerner vindicated Marx's assertions that society was economically determined, though Marx was wrong in identifying the final product—which was a central contention of the economic historian W.W. Rostow. Although Rostow's work demonstrated more of the mechanics of how a country becomes modern, it was short in its explanation of how democracy is a product of economics; he agreed with Marx and Lerner that it was economically determined, but his defense lacked particulars. Rostow believed that the secret to understanding a country's level of modernization rested with its level of technology. Traditional landholding countries had low levels of technology, hence few players in the economic and political realms.

Modern science helped to open the eyes of traditional states. They could see that economic progress was necessary. Rostow's theory asserted that economic growth is helped with the development of an effective centralized state. The state helps facilitate the growth of banks and the mobilization of capital. As the state and the private sector work together, all forces resisting economic growth are overcome. Technological abilities in industry improve drastically, and the political system makes economic development a high priority. This eventually leads to the situation where economic output is greater than the growth in population, and finally a consumer society is born. The state is then able to move resources away from economic development toward social/welfare concerns and security.[6]

Rostow's work is a form of economic determinism and is reflective of Weber in the sense that the state is developed to facilitate capitalism. But Rostow's theory placed far too much emphasis on economic determinism. Modernization and political liberty were seen as inevitable outcomes of economic development. The theory paid little attention to making connections between economic development and democratization. This problem was rectified in part by the work of Seymour Martin Lipset. Lipset's work remains highly influential in linking economic growth to democratization. He asserted that the "more well-to-do a nation, the greater the chances it will sustain democracy."[7] Lipset argued that the connection between economic development and the level of political participation needed to sustain democracy has been acknowledged from the time of Aristotle. He did not propose that economic development would result in democracy but, rather, that economics and democracy were strongly correlated because along with economic development came a level of wealth, industrialization, urbanization, and education that were all important indices of democracy. However, democracy remained highly unpredictable, even though economic development certainly improved the prospects for democracy.

Scholars became disillusioned with modernization theory and, in fact, all kinds of linear development theory that attempted to explain the prospects for democracy.[8] Besides being characterized as Western-biased, countries began to develop economically but failed to make the political transition to democracy. In some cases, countries opted to use the power of the authoritarian state to modernize the economy and hold back the forces of political liberalization. Some leaders of authoritarian states and even some scholars came to argue that the modern nation-state could include a variety of regimes and combinations of regimes and economic institutions. Hence, some states could be authoritarian but have modern economies and state bureaucracies.[9] For most comparativists interested in democratic development, modernization theory proved to be disappointing. Modernization theories were largely abandoned by the early 1970s. By the late 1980s, Lipset's work would find new acceptance, though the linkage of economics to democracy remains hotly debated. Some analysts suggest that economic development is better accomplished after or during, rather than prior to, the transition to democracy. Some even suggest that economic development can be a detriment to democracy. We will look at these arguments later in the chapter.

The most significant contribution of these early modernization theories is the widespread acceptance that, ultimately, the quality of democracy and the prospects for democratic survival are linked to economic success. This is hardly a new argument. Philosophers have been making this assertion for centuries. Lipset's contribution is that he reaffirmed this thesis and included contemporary institutions in his analysis, which has proven to be a benchmark of scholarship to many comparativists.

Political Culture Theories

Cultural analysis always has been an important component of political science. From the time of the Greek philosophers to the present, understanding culture has been considered essential if one is to understand the dynamics of a political regime. The influence of political culture studies on comparative politics cannot be underestimated, and most introductory comparative politics courses spend a considerable amount of time looking at the importance of political culture. In addition, many scholars continue to assert the primacy of political culture in their scholarship.

Recent studies suggest that political culture is perhaps more important to consider within the context of the consolidation phase of democracy.[10] Still, nearly every serious comparative study pays some attention to questions of political culture. For a time, it seemed as though studying political culture was the only way to proceed in comparative politics. Political culture studies grew in influence at the same time and, in fact, competed with modernization theories. Advocates of political culture studies argued that culture was the starting ground for understanding all political phenomena. Ultimately, not only was the prospect for democracy dependent on a nurturing culture, but modernization itself was said to be dependent on the proper cultural environment.

David Easton's work helped generate interest in political culture studies. Easton believed political scientists should spend less time looking at the state and its particular institutions and more time focusing on the political system and its processes. By system, Easton meant the political environment as a whole, not simply immediate political players or state institutions. He believed that societies (with all of their component parts) play specific political functions that shape the content of policy proposals, react to policy outcomes, and provide feedback to the state. He saw the political system as a complex interplay of factors that should be studied much the same way that a biologist studies an ecosystem. By focusing on the functions that societies perform (rather than rights and the specifics of liberalism or any other political philosophy), Easton believed we would come closer to explaining political systems. While Easton's work did not focus on political culture per se, he nevertheless assumed factors external to the government deserved the greatest attention because they shaped state structures and policies.[11]

Like Easton, Almond spent a considerable amount of effort studying political functionalism. But by the 1960s, Almond was moving away from functionalism and turning more to specific cultural characteristics of regimes. Almond and Verba are two of the most important pioneers in modern political culture studies. Their 1963 book, *The Civic Culture*, was a major success in convincing several generations of political scientists that the underlying conditions for both authoritarianism and democracy could be understood best by looking at the political culture of the country under question.[12] They defined political culture as "the particular distribution of patterns of orientation toward political objects among the members of a nation."[13] Their main concern was to find political cultures that support democracy—civic cultures. A civic culture was a mixed political culture that "stresses the participation of individuals in the political input process," characterized by a "high frequency of political activity, of exposure to political communication, of political discussion, of concern with political affairs."[14] But they cautioned that a civic culture was not civics in the "textbook" sense. In a civic culture, "political activity, involvement, and rationality exist but are balanced by passivity, traditionality, and commitment to parochial values."[15] Their interest in civic cultures grew out of a desire to understand why fascism and communism emerged at a time when democratic promise seemed so bright. They believed that rather than a simple rejection of democracy, there must be deeper, cultural reasons why some nations would embrace democracy while others would reject it. Influenced by the social science methods that were just beginning to emerge, Almond, Verba, and others began to employ various behavioral methods to assist them in their work. They believed there must be specific psychological, sociological, historical, political, and anthropological conditions that shape cultures in ways that make them either receptive to or suspicious of liberal political ideas. If social scientists could find a way to study cultures by measuring their degree of civic culture, we could gain a greater understanding of which countries are likely to be authoritarian and which countries are likely to embrace and sustain democracy. To measure civic culture, comparativists set out to look at levels of education, media exposure, religious backgrounds, ethnicity, and all other factors that would influence the attitudes, values, and habits of a particular political culture. As this information was gathered, typologies were developed that described cultural traits of authoritarianism, democracy, and countries in various stages of transition from authoritarianism to democracy.

Political culture studies took an interdisciplinary approach in order to look at a wide variety of characteristics that have relevance to regime development. The work of anthropologists, psychologists, sociologists, and economists was used to measure both the influences that *condition* cultures and those that could *change* cultures to become more receptive to democratic ways. The focus of civic culture studies primarily ascertained cultures as a whole, though there were attempts to examine the influences political leadership had on the masses.

Because the civic culture theories first studied the successful democracies of the West as a model of democratic receptiveness, some critics charged that political culture methods were flawed. Why should selecting a cultural tradition from the West be applicable to a nation-state where historical and cultural traditions varied widely from the Anglo-American model?[16] What if different conditions existed in countries that suggested that a different kind of regime besides democracy was truly preferred by the people? There were also questions about the methods used in gathering information about cultures. Many studies utilized computer-generated surveys to measure political attitudes as a way of gauging a country's political culture, but questions surfaced about the accuracy of such surveys in countries where the lack of political freedoms may prohibit honest responses,[17] and there were complaints that the questions asked were biased because they projected democratic preferences over preferences for other kinds of regimes.

Some scholars accepted the criticisms that political culture studies had been too Western-biased but decided that the importance of political culture methods was what they could tell us about attitudes toward political leadership, recruitment, media influence, education, and political socialization in a general way—not necessarily as a way to foster political ideas that may be alien to specific political cultures. As indicated in the preceding chapter, this decision led to a widespread acceptance of cultural relativism.[18] Instead of focusing on how countries could become democratic, political culture studies encouraged us to understand why countries' political cultures and regimes differed from our own. Studying political culture could teach us tolerance for other cultures and teach us to consider how some countries may be politically developed without being democratic.

To some comparativists, the heavy emphasis on political culture had gone too far. The usefulness of political culture had been overstated or had been looked at without considering the importance of political theory in general.[19] Political culture theorists had made the same methodological error the proponents of modernization theory were making. They viewed their theories as a single determinant of political reality and, in so doing, had drifted far afield from the kinds of questions on which political scientists were supposed to focus. Little attention was given to political institutions, political ideas, and democratic philosophy in general. In focusing on political attitudes and political culture at the expense of many other factors, comparativists left little room to criticize policies or leaders because they placed too much emphasis on the masses. Such questions as "What is justice?" "What is the best regime?" "What is virtue?" had been overlooked. Political culture had started out as a way to understand the conditions that made countries ripe for democracy and had ended up as a way to promote skepticism and relativism. The strong reliance on the methods of modern social science had led comparativists away from many of the concerns of political science into a malaise that nearly destroyed comparative politics as a subfield.[20] Behavioral studies focused on people's perceptions without being able to point to specific reasons why people felt the way they did, and much of the interpretation of survey material was basically guesswork. The approach did little to advance the understanding of factors that promote or threaten political stability. It lacked explanatory power because the theories were based on psychological causation rather than analysis of political systems. Political culture studies had incorporated much from the fashionable socialization theories of the day, but they could not adequately account for variation between or within cultures or between or within regimes. Consequently, political culture studies were largely abandoned from the mid-1970s to the late 1980s, as scholars turned from their attempts to explain the cultural conditions necessary for democracy toward looking at the role elites play in authoritarian and democratic regimes.

The Emergence of a Mainstream Approach

Several major studies helped move comparative politics away from the linear development model of modernization theory and the relativism and misuse of political culture studies. In 1968, Samuel Huntington published his influential book *Political Order in Changing Societies*.[21] Huntington's work had always sought balance in considering factors that lead to regime change. Though his work demonstrated concern for modernization and political culture, he called upon scholars to focus on the sources of political conflict that lead to political stability or instability. According to Huntington, comparativists need to look at social and economic change not as the engines that determine political regimes, but as catalysts that "extend political consciousness, multiply political demands, and broaden political participation." Huntington argued this focus was imperative because it was social and economic change that undermined political authority and introduced new political actors onto the scene—changes that would lead to the creation of new political institutions and regime change.[22] Huntington challenged comparativists to look at political decay, violence, and authority structures as harbingers of change. Elites, both in and out of circles of political power, should be the primary concern of comparativists because it was elites that determined the course of political conflict and compromise. Authoritarianism in all its forms, military regimes, Leninist regimes, and Praetorian regimes all had their weaknesses and were all vulnerable to decay because of domestic and foreign socioeconomic change. Huntington did not declare democracy as the only legitimate focus of development studies. Instead, he held out hope for political development by arguing that stable authoritarian regimes were more likely to limit their power than regimes where no clear political authority existed. Authoritarian regimes differed from one another in both their ability to adjust to the stresses of modernization and their capacity to liberalize.[23]

Huntington's book was as much a summary of what we knew about political change as it was a needed corrective to the drift comparative studies had made away from politics as a focus of development. His efforts were bolstered up by other scholars as well. Modernization and culture studies had contributed to development studies, but the proponents of both traditions had overestimated the importance of their theories, making culture and modernization causes of regime change, rather than single factors among many competing factors that lead to regime change. There was no single requisite to democracy; democratic development defied neat categories suggested by social requisites, be they cultural or economic.[24] By the early 1970s, the mainstream of comparative politics began to focus on leaders of authoritarian regimes and critics of the regimes who challenged authoritarians. Scholars identified patterns that emerged as particular economic and political crises challenged authoritarian regimes to retrench or liberalize. Drawing from the work of Huntington and others, scholars were able to identify general kinds of crises that gave rise to patterns of elite behavior. Crises and the way elites responded to crises encouraged comparativists to begin looking at the underlying causes of political conflict as potential factors leading to democratic compromise or increased repression.[25] While modernization theory and culture theory paid a good deal of attention to mass behavior, renewed attention focused primarily on elites. Like Huntington, scholars suggested the sources of political pressure came from such social questions as "Who is to participate in decision making?" "How well are government decisions supported?" "Is the government willing and able to control political participation?" and "How effective are government decisions and government services?" A crisis in any of these areas requires the government to innovate or undergo some sort of institutional change in order to deal with a crisis. If the system is not flexible, it has to make changes or risk collapse.[26] Some scholars were sure that political development was unlikely unless a regime had to pass through crises and, more particularly, develop institutional changes to solve the crises. Hence, unrest and regime instability were no longer considered simply bad; they were signs that an existing authoritarian regime, or a weak democratic system, had to make institutional changes in order to escape the threat of economic and political disasters. For many in political science, the refocus on elites and the state as an institution worth studying brought credibility back to comparative studies because scholars were able to study regimes without the burdens of theories that argued for the exclusiveness of economic or cultural factors in political development.

The Challenge of the Radicals

The refocus on elites and the state was a welcome relief, but regime change in authoritarian states was slow. Scholars and policymakers had become skeptical of theories advocating the prospects of democracy. By the mid-1960s and continuing well into the 1980s, a radical challenge to comparative politics emerged that had a tremendous impact on the subfield. Much of this was a reaction to modernization theory, though radicals soon took aim at culture studies, and the work of Huntington and other "traditional" comparativists as well.

Many radicals shared a common point of departure with Rostow, that is, they believed an economic focus was the proper starting point for understanding problems of political development. However, the radicals actually shared more in common with Marxist theories of economic determinism than with Rostow's revised Weberian approach. Simply put, radicals argued that, rather than serving as an engine of growth, capitalism was actually an agent that discouraged or prevented balanced economic growth and therefore promoted authoritarianism in the periphery. To be sure, many Marxist scholars argued this point all through

42

the latter part of the nineteenth century and throughout the twentieth century. The difference, however, was that this view was finding acceptance among a whole generation of scholars. One scholar's work was particularly influential in encouraging radical scholarship. Andre Gunder Frank suggested that capitalism led to the development of underdevelopment.[27] In other words, he believed the same processes that led to the successful development of a particular sector of the economy also led to the underdevelopment of other sectors of the economy. He developed ideas that came to be referred to as "dependency theory." He suggested that as center countries (or in his terms, *the metropole*) interacted with economic elites in the periphery (or *satellite*), they would find mutual economic benefits through trade and development projects. Those lacking direct links to the center, however, not only were closed off from economic development, but were prevented from being able to enjoy the rewards of capitalist development. Hence, capitalism was dangerous not simply because it failed to distribute wealth evenly, but because it created conditions that made it even more difficult for those who are marginalized to ever benefit from the existing economic order. The political regime was geared toward continuing its economic links with the center; hence, political change was not likely to occur. A few mainstream comparativists, including Guillermo O'Donnell, were influenced by this general trend in scholarship. O'Donnell feared that modernization's impact in Argentina and Brazil was to build and strengthen authoritarian structures rather than mobilizing forces to remove them. He feared that a wave of authoritarianism could be expected in many Latin American regimes unless economic development could be implemented in a way to encourage liberalization and democracy.[28] The difference between a typical authoritarian regime and a bureaucratic-authoritarian regime was that the latter was more stable and permanent because of its institutional development and links to external capital resources and economic development. Infusions of money from banks, governments, and industries in wealthy countries brought great pressure upon populist governments. In order to meet the demands of these sources of capital, technocrats with the backing of militaries took power, creating bureaucratic-authoritarian regimes. Power was very often distributed among an elite group rather than a single authoritarian leader. Because no single ruler could be held responsible in such a system, O'Donnell feared a bureaucratic-authoritarian regime could persist longer than a conventional authoritarian regime.

Radicals built on Frank's work. Dependency theorists forwarded many variations to Frank's thesis, though most were in agreement that international capitalism was the culprit that led to harsh authoritarian regimes. Instead of supporting the Marxist contention that democracy kept capitalism going through a series of reforms and laws to sustain capitalist expansion, dependency theorists argued that authoritarians kept economic resources at their disposal through their monopoly of political power. Some theorists argued that in many cases political regimes were not ruled simply by particular leaders, but by a combination of domestic leaders seeking foreign trade and international capitalists who sought to maintain favorable economic conditions. Industrialization could, and did, occur in dependent countries as technology was transferred from rich countries to select regions in poor countries. This kind of development made good economic sense for the elites of poor countries and the elites in the rich countries with whom they traded, but the masses in poor, dependent countries would feel no relief and would have their economic conditions deteriorate as this dependent relationship between the center and periphery continued.[29] If economic elites could maintain political power, they could continue to maintain the pattern of economic development and underdevelopment.

The radicals critiqued not only modernization theory, but also culture theories and the work of mainstream theorists. The political culture proponents and mainstream comparativists were criticized not so much for the detail of their work, but more because they had failed to take an economic focus to their work. The problem with scholars who failed to take an economic focus was that their work underestimated how important economics, particularly international capitalism, was to the whole problem of political development. Almond, Huntington, and others failed to see that economic conditions determined the rules for all other concerns of policy and political and social science in general.[30]

Some radicals suggested that criticisms of political culture theory and modernization theory had not gone far enough. Political culture and modernization theories were incorrect, and even the work of those who previously had criticized these theories for being biased was incorrect because they had used traditional Western categories of analysis to inform their criticisms. Thus, the culprit was assuming that political culture was based on Western assumptions. In fact, it was the whole project of Western social science that had left scholars with only a handful of ideal-type categories, which encouraged comparativists to presume that all societies wanted essentially the same things. In particular, comparativists too often assumed that all forms of authoritarianism were the same regardless of whether they were Western or not. Western political philosophy, Western social science, and the radical approaches were all based on ethnocentric beliefs about human behavior and did much to encourage foreign policies that supported the Western bias in international politics. What comparativists needed to do was to look at how non-Western scholars and policymakers went about studying questions of political development. By using the same terms and concepts, comparativists—whether they be radicals, modernization proponents, political culture theorists, or traditionalists—really promoted a unilateral assumption of development, based on the belief that Western analysis of regime quality is correct. These radical critics believed that distinctively Asian, African, and Latin American theories of development could challenge the condescending views held by scholars in the United States and Western Europe.[31]

Which Approach Is Best?

The methods used by early comparativists have all been useful to a certain degree, but there are weaknesses within each approach, and there are general problems that all of them hold in common. It is useful at this point to offer a critique of each approach.

Political Culture Theory

The bias that early political culture theorists held toward democracy is a good one. It is unfortunate that many who subscribed to the political culture method abandoned their advocacy of democracy in favor of regimes that claimed to be more in keeping with the cultural traditions of individual countries. A careful reading of political philosophy reveals nondemocratic regimes tend to fit certain patterns that philosophers have identified through the centuries. Hence, there actually are no new regime types, only variations on the kinds of regimes we already know about.

The problem that plagues political culture studies is one that has plagued social science for some time. Modern social science is based on positivist assumptions that came into vogue with the behavioralist revolution of the 1950s and 1960s. The reliance on the scientific method and computers to process great amounts of information did not get to the

45

source of the problem behind modern social science methodologies—
that being the assumption social scientists made. At the time that ideal
typologies were being discussed by Max Weber and other early social
scientists, philosophers like Edmund Husserl were warning that social
science methods were flawed because the underlying assumptions of
positivist science were flawed and contradictory.[32] Husserl pointed to
the gross errors that social science had made in following the methods
that natural scientists blindly use to "uncover truths." Natural and social
scientists, enamored with the desire to find objective truths, turned to
empirical evidence to verify their theses. While this is often the source
of inaccuracy in natural science, social scientists end up making absurd
observations in order to substantiate universal claims. But the fundamental assumptions about objectivity—absolute truth and empirical
facts—lead to the projection of initial assumptions as truths in and of
themselves. Then when general observation reveals that the empirical
evidence is not accurate, social scientists become skeptical of their find-
ings. They reject all science as value laden, a priori understandings of
phenomena that may or may not relate to truth. Skepticism and relativism wins the day, and all truth is discounted or entirely rejected.

Such is an adequate description of the assumptions made by many
who advocated political culture studies. When empirical evidence (the
development of conditions favorable for democracy) did not support
actual events (a continuation of or return to authoritarianism), political scientists became discouraged and skeptical of social science inquiry. Instead, they became advocates of cultural relativism and,
therefore, apologists for authoritarianism. Their mistakes became the
fodder for the canons of the radicals and others who suggested that
political culture studies had promised an understanding of democracy
but in the end contributed nothing. If comparativists had viewed political culture as one aspect of democracy, criticism would not have
been as harsh. While some of this criticism has been warranted, political culture has once again proven to be an important focus for comparative politics, just as it has for others who have studied cultural aspects of
authoritarianism and democracy through the centuries; political culture
is but one aspect, albeit an important one to consider, in the democratization process. But the claims political culture made suggesting that
culture is the main determinant of a country's ability to democratize and
maintain democracy are simplistic. Comparativists need to be more eclec-
tic and careful in their analysis. While truths exist, boldly identifying

truths as concrete objects that can be studied without understanding the assumptions we bring to social science inquiry is dangerous and does more to promote relativism than the truths we seek to realize.

Modernization Theory

Any social science methodology that asserts the primacy of a single underlying factor that determines the character of a political society is going to invite widespread criticism. Like political culture theory, modernization theory seeks an underlying causal factor for determining political development. And like political culture theory, when the empirical evidence proved to be too divergent from real economic and political events, relativism set in. Some modernization theorists abandoned liberal democracy proclaiming "people's democracy" or other hybrid authoritarian systems that promoted economic growth to be developed political systems.[33]

Modernization theory makes the same errors Marxism makes. It argues that political and other social aspects of life are merely a product of economic conditions. Economic success is seen as the primary goal of the state and of individuals within the state. Again the evidence of developing states suggests that while it is true that economics matters a great deal during regime transitions and democratic consolidation, there are other factors that can have even greater importance than economic ones in the success of the regime. The underlying assumptions modernization theorists often made were simple cause/effect relationships in the economic realm. They attempted to isolate economic activity as the sole criterion of political change and therefore lost sight of the goals of liberalism, which are vast and include far more than economic modernization.

Economics is nevertheless a very important focus of development studies. Economic hope is linked to democratic aspirations all over the world. Democracy and economic development are important partners, but the actual relationship of economics to democracy is not adequately understood within the confines of a simple theoretical framework, be it Marxist or non-Marxist. This is where studies such as those by Montesquieu and Tocqueville are most helpful in guiding us toward responsible analysis of economic and political factors and how they relate to democracy and authoritarianism. Montesquieu argued that a liberal economic system provided a realm for citizens to practice self-rule. A commercial republic allowed for a complex interplay of laws and liberties that would teach people to love their freedoms and their republic. In addition to being a nursery for democracy, the economic realm was also an outlet for people to satisfy material desires that cannot be satisfied in any other way. Montesquieu understood that political and economic freedoms provided the conditions necessary for promoting economic development. Similarly, Tocqueville believed a commercial republic would allow people to practice their self-interest in a guarded way. Laws and virtues would balance overemphasis on the drive for wealth. The economic system would teach moderation and compromise in order to sustain economic rules that would benefit all. These considerations are not well developed in the modernization literature.

The Radical Approach

The radical approach to studying development and underdevelopment suffers from the same problems as modernization theory. Instead of exaggerating the connection of economic development to democratization, radical theorists exaggerated the negative effects of capitalist development and the maintenance of authoritarian regimes. While the radicals criticized modernization theorists for being naive in their simple assumptions, they committed a more serious error. Why this sharp criticism? Because while modernization theorists overestimated the impact economic growth would have on political development, radical theories have proven to be too pessimistic in predicting the development patterns and staying power of authoritarian regimes. Many radical case studies suggested countries in Latin America and Asia were doomed to authoritarian legacies because of the role of multinational corporations and external capitalist development in general. The masses were said to be cut out of economic and political participation because those who were connected to the sources of capital controlled the political arena. There is evidence that this trend is changing, though Latin American countries have not been as successful as East Asian countries in promoting balanced economic development. Some of these countries have rejected authoritarianism and made the transition to democracy but seem to be failing at consolidating democracy. Others have made the transition to democracy without making significant changes in their economic systems until democratic leaders implemented new economic policies.[34] But the problems are more far-reaching than strictly economic. Scholars are increasingly skeptical of the radical approach to studying these countries and believe more mainstream approaches to studying the region will tell us more about the problems these countries face.[35]

As far as the criticism that social science and policymakers are Western-biased, more comparativists are less worried about such accusations than they were in the past. Examining our assumptions about democracy and social inquiry in general has reassured us that democracy is a worthy goal to seek and that Western scholarship provides the best means to date by which to study regimes. The so-called social sciences of non-Western cultures have been abandoned by non-Westerners, especially as social scientists and social reformers all over the world advocate democracy.

Early Mainstream Approaches

Scholars who avoided the single-cause explanations of political development have found their work has greater staying power. They have employed traditional social science models and tend to share a common belief about the significance of liberal democracy as a goal of development. While political culture theory, modernization theory, and radical theory have made contributions to development studies, the more "orthodox" mainstream approach to studying political development has greater explanatory power and has survived the test of time. This assessment of success is based on the growth of democratic literature that has continued into the present day and because mainstream scholars have done the most important work in refocusing the concerns of comparative politics on democracy. Although this approach includes scholars who are divided over the relative importance of various ideas and theories, they have been the most outspoken defenders of democracy as a benchmark of development. Their criticism of authoritarianism has kept them focused on the ways countries democratize. They have been more willing to borrow ideas from a variety of other approaches without fear of watering down their own theoretical positions. This is not to say that mainstream scholars have been perfect in their studies of political development, but their work has been more successful in transcending historical trends, complaints about cultural bias, and specific methodological controversies. This interest has kept development studies alive as it has helped us understand the processes at work in regimes that have resulted in successful transitions to democracy.

In some cases, mainstream comparativists reinvented the wheel as far as studies of democracy are concerned. The emphasis on looking at elites in liberalizing systems, the processes of conflict and compromise, and philosophical support for democracy have always been considered of key importance to political philosophers who have studied democracy.[36] The impact of social science methodology drove comparative politics away from democratic philosophy and left us ill equipped to understand political events that hinted of democratic change. The third wave of democracy (see ch. 1, n. 29) is telling in this respect. While many countries began their transition to democracy, radical theorists were enjoying their greatest acceptance. Comparativists were reluctant to accept democracy as the regime of choice. As a result, scholarship lagged behind the third wave of democracy, emerging well after the third wave had slowed. Comparativists were caught by surprise. What people were studying stood in stark contrast to what was actually occurring in the world. Greater attention to democratic philosophy would not necessarily have resulted in our ability to predict that a new wave of democracy was under way but it would have helped us analyze more fully the democratic transitions that were going on and assess the quality of regimes that were consolidating. We would have been better prepared to consider questions regarding liberty, equality, and justice in liberalizing regimes and utilize the rich tradition of democratic theory we have at our disposal.

Contemporary Mainstream Theory About Transitions

Even though the mainstream approach to studying democratic transitions has prevailed, major points of disagreement exist within the mainstream camp. In addition, an interest has been rekindled in modernization theory and in political culture theory, though both of these approaches are making quieter and less grandiose claims. Mainstream theorists like Samuel Huntington have developed theoretical sketches that attempt to explain the global phenomenon of democratization in the late twentieth century. Others like Larry Diamond and Alfred Stepan point to the peculiar nature of democratization as it presents itself in individual cases. Still, they generally agree that several factors are of vital importance in studying democratic transitions. Focusing on elites in the transition process and looking at how democratic compromises are negotiated are both seen as primary factors in understanding the transition process. Agreeing that these two components are essential to understanding transitions, however, is not the same as suggesting that this is where one should begin in considering democratic transitions.

How to Begin?

How does one begin to understand the underlying factors behind a transition? This question is not merely one of deciding if "the chicken or the egg came first"; it throws comparative politics back into the debates of the past. While some scholars agree that elites negotiating regime change is the basis of the transition process, others believe that specific conditions give rise to the development of a political elite to debate these issues—which takes us back to our old quarrel about prerequisites to democracy.

It was stated previously that most scholars believed that prerequisites arguments, be they modernization theories or theories of political culture, overstated the relative importance of their tenets in clearing the way for democracy. It was also noted, however, that both political culture and economic modernization are important factors to consider in the transition from authoritarianism to democracy. Scholars recognized that no political transitions have spontaneous beginnings, that something has to act as a catalyst for democratization. So what is it that starts democratic transitions?

Most scholars believe transitions begin when there is a growing feeling within an existing regime that the current leadership may not be able to cope with existing or potential crises. In their famous study on transitions from authoritarianism, O'Donnell and Schmitter assert that "there is no transition whose beginning is not the consequence—direct or indirect—of important divisions within the authoritarian regime itself, principally along the fluctuating cleavage between hard-liners and soft-liners."[37] What are these crises that create the cleavages between hard-liners and soft-liners? What effect do elites and nonelites outside the regime who challenge authoritarianism altogether have on the leadership?

O'Donnell and Schmitter suggest that any number of domestic factors can initiate regime disintegration, though they believe policy failure in general promotes a split within the ruling regime. Hard-liners support exclusionary policies while soft-liners are more willing to experiment with liberal reforms. Outside opposition movements grow, which may give soft-liners power to negotiate reforms, or encourage hard-liners to purge critics in and out of the regime. An opposition movement may be disorganized and lack an effective leader, which will have little or no impact on the existing regime and therefore play no immediate role in the transition process. While O'Donnell and Schmitter prefer to focus on general policy crises as catalysts for regime change, others suggest there is a wide range of specific factors that encouraged the third wave of democracy.

Conditions that Create Political Crises

Huntington identifies five factors that prepare an environment for transition from authoritarianism to democracy. These factors do not occur by accident but constitute five independent variables that bring stress to existing authoritarian regimes and thereby create conditions that lead to reform movements.[38]

Legitimacy Problems of Authoritarian Regimes

Authoritarian regimes that are unable to satisfactorily address crises lose their legitimacy. Scholars have noted that sooner or later authoritarian ideology is no longer able to justify all political and economic policy. As authoritarian ideology fails, legitimacy can be regained only by success in policy formulation and implementation.[39] A regime that is successful in policy formulation but weak in political ideas eventually risks its legitimacy because it is not able to define political goals and convince elites in and out of the regime why it should maintain exclusive control of political decisionmaking. Additionally, policy failure that has no political base or a weak political base can result in a rapid loss of legitimacy. Some scholars do not believe that economic disaster is reason enough for a regime to disintegrate, but they do believe poor economic conditions undermine support for authoritarian regimes—and there is broad agreement that a loss of legitimacy, whether for economic or political reasons, often convinces leaders that no regime other than a democratic one can be legitimized.[40]

Global Economic Growth

Lipset's theory (discussed earlier in this chapter) finds some applicability in recent scholarship on transitions. In addition, Huntington finds modernization theory valid in terms of its suggestion that economic modernization has led to higher education levels, increased mobility, higher living standards, and the growth of middle classes living in authoritarian states. This has created conditions helpful for the growth of opposition movements and calls for reform in and out of authoritarian regimes.

Religious Reform

As a result of Vatican II, the Roman Catholic Church has become an active advocate of social reform. Democracy is supported as a virtue, and authoritarianism is criticized as an inferior regime. However, some scholars are not convinced that religious reform has had an even effect on the prospects for a democratic transition.[41] Even though the Catholic Church officially encourages democracy, local church leaders vary greatly from country to country in their advocacy of democratic reform.

The successful transition to democracy in several Confucian countries has demonstrated that Confucian tenets are not as much of a barrier to democracy as previously believed. While certain aspects of Confucianism undoubtedly influence the political cultures of East Asian countries, the attractiveness of democracy seems to transcend the authoritarian attributes of Confucianism.[42] Some scholars even suggest Confucianism is a partner in democratic development.[43] The same is not generally said about Islam. Islam tends to support regimes that uphold the authority of Islamic law. For this reason, many scholars believe Islam is antithetical to democracy.[44]

Role of External Actors

The adoption of democratic norms among international organizations and the promotion of democracy by international bodies is seen not only as educating leaders of authoritarian regimes, but also as encouraging elites to organize opposition movements that seek measured change. Many scholars have noted the encouraging role that such organizations as the European Economic Council (EEC) have played in rewarding membership benefits to countries making democratic reforms (as well as their role in withholding benefits from countries maintaining authoritarianism).[45]

The downfall of communist states has also contributed to the democratic spirit. The collapse of the Soviet Union removed an important impediment to political reform in Eastern Europe and in other parts of the world. As communism continues to collapse, the political prospects for democracy may increase if it becomes apparent to elites within (and opponents to) regimes that communism, and authoritarianism in general, is not a viable alternative to democracy.

Demonstration Effects

As nations embrace democracy, remaining authoritarian regimes lag behind. Authoritarian nations increase their democratic rhetoric and begin to move toward a democratic compromise in order to avoid this trend. Leaders start to think about their legacies and do not want to be known as the last authoritarian rulers of their respective countries. Hence, few leaders continue to argue for the superiority of authoritarianism over democracy.

All of these factors, according to Huntington, create conditions that force authoritarian regimes to undergo fundamental reform. However, they are unable to handle such wide and significant challenges adequately, and in their attempt to survive, they develop new institutions that resemble those found in democratic states. In making these changes the transition process begins. The transition to democracy may be successful, it may stop short of establishing liberal tenets necessary to create a bona fide democracy, or it may collapse into authoritarianism again. Much is dependent on the skill of those negotiating political change—which brings us back once again to the key role played by elites.

Who Are the Elites, and What Do They Argue About?

As indicated at the outset of this chapter, it is a common belief that because democracy is government "of the people, by the people, and for the people," it is therefore *created* "by the people." However, democratic transitions start with elites seeking negotiated settlements. Popular revolutions are frequently unsuccessful and can easily doom the prospects for a democratic transition because wars, violent acts, and popular participation in the transition process often make compromise difficult. The institutional capacities of elites to keep government services running, make policies to address problems, and organize elections and other institutions to represent society can easily be forgotten in a country where popular insurrection exists. It is often difficult for leaders and participants of mass movements to recognize that smooth, orderly transitions vastly improve the prospects for democratic behavior both before and after the first popular elections. If elements of the old government can have a hand in shaping the new democratic regime, the prospects for democracy may be greatly enhanced. This is because former authoritarians have a personal stake in the success of a regime they have helped build. It is less likely that former opponents will fight against democracy, even after having to step down from their privileged positions of power, if they or their associates have been involved in the discussions to introduce democracy.

Sultanist Authoritarian Regimes

Some authoritarian leaders refuse to submit to a democratic compromise, especially if they held a great deal of personal power in the previous regime. Referring to this type of autocratic government as a "sultanist regime," Linz and Stepan point out that because the power base is centered on the leader individually, he or she may have to be thrown out of office by armed force, assassination, exile, or some other drastic measure that raises the risks of a successful democratic transition.[46] The more stability elites can bring to the transition process, the greater the chances of long-term success in the consolidation process because habits of compromise and negotiation become institutionalized early in the overall democratization process.

Because sultanistic regimes usually include few people in the decision-making process, few elites have proven track records in promoting reform. This increases uncertainty in the transition process. Typical authoritarian regimes have cliques or factions that can be associated with particular policies or reforms. This helps identify potential allies and enemies of democracy. Because sultanistic regimes are quite closed, there is also the question of whether or not associates of the deposed leader can claim enough support for a democratic transition. Opposition leaders generally mistrust former members of sultanistic regimes, primarily because they have been associated with brutal leaders and their political positions are largely unknown. For these reasons, once a transition takes place, sultanistic regimes have proven to be resistant to change and are not as easily consolidated as nonsultanist regimes.

Regimes Led by Military Leaders

Military leaders may or may not hinder the prospects for a democratic transition. Hierarchical military regimes may have some of the same attributes as sultanistic regimes. Power may be concentrated by a single military leader or group; however, security is tight in the hierarchical regime. Opponents can be jailed, tortured, or killed. But many military regimes can accept a civilian role in government, especially in areas where particular expertise (e.g., economic development) is needed. Here the military comes to share power over time with other groups in the government. Some military regimes actually lose much of their military character and eventually become civilian authoritarian regimes.[47] It is not impossible for military regimes to resign from the new government if they see that greater expertise is needed, or if the costs of repression are greater than the costs of allowing a new regime to take over.[48] In many cases, military regimes are also tied to political parties. Some military governments actually share power with, or even get their political power from, a ruling political party. This can improve the prospects for a transition if civilian members of the party can encourage greater civilian representation in the government, assume operation of the government, and take the lead in negotiating a transition. In some cases, military leaders see the advantage of separating themselves from political parties and playing the role of protector of the state rather than performing functions of state security and law enforcement.

Some military regimes are led by young officers who are not a part of the upper military command. They have taken power by a coup d'etat and generally play a temporary role; they find it difficult to maintain power because competing military leaders are always a threat. The young officer's goal is often to replace a government with whom he disagrees, not necessarily to serve as the new political master of the country. Hence, these military regimes are not usually long-lived, and their leaders are usually anxious to work out a compromise.

In communist regimes, military leaders have been brought in ruling circles as a way to maintain power over the military. In these cases, militaries tend to play a less important role in the transition process than political leaders.

Totalitarian Regimes

Former communist regimes do present problems that other authoritarian systems do not in the transition from authoritarian rule. Even though the communist party may be disbanded and significant progress is made to liberalize the system, previous ways of handling political affairs can continue to haunt former communist countries. Even though democratic institutions have been developing in Russia, the office of the presidency of Russia has developed institutions of its own that duplicate, and in real ways undermine, the democratic institutions that seek to make laws or oversee policy implementation. While this is common in many authoritarian regimes that are becoming democratized, it is a particular problem for former totalitarian regimes because force of habit has convinced leaders that political work is accomplished by restricting the circle of political authority rather than broadening it. Skills possessed by former bureaucrats of the communist regime are needed to keep government services going, but the tactics used by these officials may slow or corrupt the transition process.

Sometimes entire bureaucracies may need to be purged, which could leave a liberalizing system without suitable administrators to guide changes through. It is common for government officials who were local and regional leaders under a communist regime to benefit financially and politically from corruption and nepotism as discipline breaks down in a rapidly changing system. Corruption undermines reform and increases frustration at a time when popular expectations demand success from democratic reforms. Former leaders can make comebacks, sometimes advocating a return to communism, or they identify new enemies of the state and advocate fascism or other extreme political fixes that challenge the pace of liberal reforms—hence, the importance of leaders who can keep democratic reform alive by adapting to changing conditions, deal with corruption, and continually promote a vision of what democratic life can be like.

Other Authoritarian Regimes

Noncommunist, one-party authoritarian regimes, and authoritarian regimes where a number of people work together to maintain political control have tended to offer the greatest chance of transitional success toward democracy. Because leadership responsibility tends to be dispersed, no single leader can operate to the exclusion of all others. This means that individual leaders are responsible for particular sectors of the government and specific policies. Because leaders shoulder responsibilities for specific ministries or policies, they recruit specialists to help them succeed, thus introducing more adaptability in policymaking and policy implementation. Their jobs require that they have success in policy implementation and that they earn some degree of public approval.

The typical authoritarian regime is a modern regime in that it employs complex economic theories, utilizes sophisticated methods to gather and process information, facilitates development, seeks public approval, and disseminates information in order to foster cooperation between the private sector and the state. Because there is some degree of pluralism in these kinds of authoritarian regimes, opposition groups find it easier to organize and are usually treated with more respect than are opposition groups in totalitarian, sultanistic, or hierarchical military regimes. In authoritarian regimes that are less severe, there is a greater chance for discussing disagreements, which creates the contradictions necessary to facilitate debate within the government. Government leaders then seek outside experts to increase their information base and back individual positions. Leaders may solicit the help of technocrats to support policies related to economics and industrialization. Later, scholars are called upon to legitimize reforms and support measures that will liberalize the system. Usually such states are not consumed with silencing opponents but seek success and security. Scholarship has shown that they are the kinds of authoritarian regimes that are most likely to cut their losses and opt for a democratic solution once they see their regime lacks long-term political promise.

The Timing of Democratic Transitions

The trick for democratizers in any regime is to determine when to seek democratic compromise. In some cases, it may not be desirable for pro-democratic leaders to take control immediately after an authoritarian regime begins to decay. It is not uncommon for the failed policies of infant democratic regimes to lead to a rejection of democracy by the critics of democracy. Many infant democracies have reverted to authoritarianism after the new democratic government proved no more or less able to improve conditions than did its predecessor. Sometimes allowing soft-liners from within the ruling regime to introduce reforms may pave the way for a smooth transition. In reforming the system, authoritarian leaders may be seeking to stay in power by staving off critics of the regime. Their ability to stay in power may be dependent on their abilities to introduce reforms. Some of these reforms may be successful while others may not. The important thing is that reforms have been attempted, and new players have been introduced to the political scene. The system has undergone a limited degree of liberalization. When this happens, there is usually no more politics as usual for the authoritarian regime. In opting for reforms, policies, or new political institutions, political leaders legitimize reform movements. Soft-liners and regime opponents gain importance, and the arena of political debate is often widened to include experts outside of government who can advise on specific policies. There is a considerable amount of contextual learning that elites acquire in the process. Hard-liners usually make an effort to rein in political reforms, retire, or throw their support behind some or all of the reforms. Soft-liners may attempt to slow reforms in order to hold on to power as long as they can, or they may become outspoken advocates of democracy. In some cases, their rhetoric may be driven by opportunistic desires but in the long run may determine to a great extent the direction they must follow.

Opposition leaders come to realize that it may be impossible and even undesirable to remove government leaders from office without negotiated agreement. They learn to trust some members of the government in order to win trust in return. Democratic gains are made. Setbacks may be long-term but are often only temporary. With time, leaders of the regime instituting reforms and opposition leaders both realize that liberalization is occurring and democratic institutions are a logical alternative.[49] Political parties come to play a major role. They institutionalize the gains made as the system has liberalized, as they have realized that political decisions must be made by collaboration, cooperation, and compromise in order to keep the democratic agenda moving. Parties limit the power of individuals and increase the chances that political issues are deliberated and debated carefully. Not all political parties increase the prospects for democracy, however. If political parties have moderate political agendas, they tend to routinize democratic gains. Extreme leftist and rightist parties that hold on to political views tend to undermine democratic gains. They exaggerate political differences and appeal to quick fixes rather than carefully deliberated programs.

Economic Success or Failure?

At any time in the transition process, policy performance shapes the direction and speed of the transition. This is especially true of economic policy. If the ruling authoritarian regime is having economic success, it may enjoy plenty of legitimacy and its position may seem secure. Calls for further reform may go unheeded, as the regime continues to bask in the success of a growing economy; but the experience of newly democratizing countries suggests that economic policy success may not be enough to keep authoritarianism going and in some cases may actually promote democratic change. Case studies indicate that economic success can eventually lead to calls for greater inclusion in the political and economic policymaking process. Liberalization usually increases the prospects of economic growth. This is true not only in terms of economic modernization, but also political modernization. The experiences of the former authoritarian regimes of Taiwan and South Korea suggest that economic success alone could neither calm the calls for increased political freedom, nor convince business leaders that authoritarian control would ensure a stable economic environment.[50] It is a lesson that some suggest is being learned in Mexico as stable economic growth and modest, though significant, political reforms have resulted in fair elections and renewed hope for a viable democratic republic.[51] Democracy can be viewed as the natural and normal complement to economic success by elites and nonelites and encourages public accountability and entrepreneurial opportunity in developing and developed countries. Where economic problems are most likely to be a setback to democracy is when pro-democratic leaders take power and are not able to enjoy economic success, or more importantly, if their economic policies backfire and economic hardship is increased. The degree of policy failure is magnified if economic success was deemed greater under a previous authoritarian regime and economic failure is associated with advocates of democracy. Sometimes reformers are too ambitious and create economic turmoil rather than promoting steady change. A lack of economic success may not even be the fault of democratizers. Economies are complex entities that make prediction difficult. Hence any number of factors, such as natural disaster, lingering problems associated with the previous regime, changes in the international economy, or countless other challenges may result in economic stagnation or decline. An infant democratic regime may be blamed for economic problems that could undermine its ability to consolidate democratic gains.

Economic problems can greatly help in the transition from authoritarianism to democracy, however. If an authoritarian regime has been able to enjoy some economic success, particularly in improving the standard of living, failing economic policies may help convince authoritarians that the risks of maintaining authoritarianism outweigh the trouble of opting for democracy. If a transition occurs in part because of economic hardship, democratic reformers do themselves a favor by attempting to lower the expectations of the people and in trying to educate people about the difficulties that they must face in the future if democracy and long-term economic success are to be realized. As Linz and Stepan have pointed out, these tactics have proven to be helpful in countries like Spain, Portugal, and Greece, as leaders attempted to gain support for democracy first, in the hopes that it will buy them enough time to weather economic uncertainty and eventually realize economic success.[52]

Bringing the People Along

In the contemporary international political climate, the lack of political freedom authoritarian regimes afford is considered to be a major factor in the failing support for authoritarianism. Even with economic success some authoritarian regimes find it increasingly difficult to maintain support. Hence many policies are seen by opposition leaders as poor substitutes for democracy. It is not unusual for democratic reformers to be far more enthusiastic about democracy than the citizenry. People tend to fear change, especially changes that bring about a regime with which they are unfamiliar. This is why it helps to have experienced elites who understand the importance of working together to broker the transition process all the way toward the first free elections and beyond into the consolidation process. It also helps if a country's neighbors are stable democracies, or at the very least, are experimenting with democratic reforms on their own and enjoying some success. Support from international organizations and important countries like the United States also increases the stature of pro-democracy leaders who are shouldered with the burden of convincing both political leaders who eschew democracy, and the masses who are unsure of and have reservations about democracy. Once again, political parties play a vital role in popularizing democratic policies and educating the public on democratic gains and policy options.

Holding Elections

For many observers, a country's first freely contested national elections mark the successful completion in the transition from authoritarianism to democracy. The agreement to convoke democratic elections is an im-

61

portant benchmark in the democratization process. Though elections do not guarantee future democratic success, elections are nevertheless a reason for advocates of democracy to celebrate. Still, the period of the founding elections in a democratic society is a very anxious moment in the transition process.[53] It is an important juncture where democratic gains can begin to be consolidated or lost depending on the entire election process and the behavior of pro-democratic and anti-democratic elites.

The logic of elections usually does not have to be taught. People understand that the idea of democratic elections is to select representatives of whom the people approve. People sense that they have been entrusted to take some responsibility in the direction they want their country to go. There is much symbolism in elections in that they are also seen as a repudiation of previous political regimes. Though they may be voting in democratic elections for the first time, the people are usually not novices when it comes to elections. In most cases, the citizenry has had some experience with elections under authoritarianism. Indeed, elections have been a mainstay of political activity in the twentieth century regardless of the type of regime in power. Communist states, one-party authoritarian states, military regimes, monarchies, and sultanistic regimes hold elections. Obviously there are different reasons for holding elections and the relative importance of elections vary greatly. But having participated in the voting process under authoritarianism is helpful in that people come to expect that their word ought to count and that elections should be routine. Irregular elections held in Mexico, Taiwan, and South Korea prior to the establishment of democracy are seen as having played a positive role in building a legitimate role for elections that would reflect popular will. In each of these cases, fraudulent elections were eventually replaced with fair elections and opposition figures were elected to the presidency of each country.[54] Hence even thrown elections or elections where the slate is set by the authoritarian elite can play an important role in future democratic participation. Scholars have found that democratic rhetoric and practices such as holding elections can help convince people that democratic ideals are important. In addition, leaders sometimes find themselves bound by what they hoped would be token attempts to placate the political opposition. Instead, they find even scripted elections raise democratic aspirations.[55]

In order for an election to be democratic, there must be high certainty that the people are given a real choice of candidates and that candidates have competed fairly for the privilege of running for office. There must

be guarantees that the people's wishes will be respected in that the win-
ner is selected by rules that are fair, and elected leaders will, in fact, be
vested with effective governing power. Sometimes elections will be held
to elect only local leaders, or heads of government, with assembly elections to follow at a later date. Initial democratic elections may vary greatly
from the elections that follow in that a regular procedure for elections
may be determined after democratic leaders take office and are able to
formally work through constitutional issues.

In some cases, former authoritarians win democratically contested elections. They may have greater financial resources backing them, or they
may be popular enough to win the elections on their own merit. Huntington suggests the real determination of whether or not elections are the
harbinger of democracy is if there is a two-turnover test.[56] By this he
means if leaders who won the first democratic elections are defeated in a
subsequent election and voluntarily step aside, the chances for democratic consolidation increase. Sometimes leaders are elected but refuse
to step down when the electorate votes for a different set of leaders in the
next election. Others win elections and then cancel or postpone future
elections in order to maintain power. Such a phenomenon is not uncommon and has been a key reason for the breakdown of democracy.[57] In
some cases, leaders attempt to convince political elites and the public
that the country faces serious problems that can only be handled by nondemocratic means. Presidents Alberto Fujimori of Peru and Carlos Menem
of Argentina have made this argument. Although claiming to go by democratic rules, both were successful in reversing democratic gains in order
to "fix" certain economic and political problems.

Usually authoritarians who run for elective office are not successful.
They are turned away because their legitimacy has already been called
into question prior to a democratic compromise. In some cases, the people
vote for other candidates because they detest the former leaders and find
repudiation at the ballot box to be the strongest official message they
can send these former leaders. Fearing electoral defeat, authoritarians
sometimes attempt to throw initial elections, postpone them, or take
some other measures to sabotage the election process. These tactics are
no longer as successful in staying the tide of democracy as they used to
be because the hunger for and success of democratic transitions brings
condemnation at home and abroad against those who oppose democratic
elections. Democratic leaders can make it easier for authoritarians to
agree to electoral rules by offering amnesty to key leaders and their

associates for crimes committed if they agree to a democratic compact. Although such an agreement is painful, especially when the people may view such an agreement as capitulation, it can make the difference between reaching a democratic agreement and thwarting democratic efforts altogether.[58]

A Critique of the Mainstream Perspective of Democratic Transitions

Recent theories of political development are far more complex and much better at explaining democratic transitions than earlier comparative theories. There has been a maturity reached in the discipline that has enabled us to understand that searching for ideal-type answers in the democratization process is futile. We appreciate that there are many factors that play important roles in the overall transition process. Recent scholarship has enabled us to put together a body of theory that is quite useful in explaining the mechanics of authoritarian regimes in transit to democracy. We can identify factors that help smooth a country's path to democracy, and we know what endangers successful transitions. We are much improved in our abilities to explain why some transitions took the paths they traveled, why some transitions were relatively easy, why others were difficult, and why some transitions failed to produce democracy altogether.

At the same time, our ability to explain the transition process is handicapped simply because we have a limited perspective. We focus primarily on elites. These elites may or may not have a significant political role in the transition process due to various environmental factors. Particular elites could be drawn in or excluded from the negotiations and activities surrounding transitions. This is because particular policy outcomes, economic circumstances, religious and cultural conditions, international actors, and related changes or crises come together to create circumstances where some elites gain in relative importance in the political give-and-take compared to others. Given the circumstances and options, elites join forces as hard-liners who seek to maintain the existing regime, soft-liners who favor guarded change, or opposition leaders who favor regime replacement or at least significant reforms that those in power oppose. Through a process of bargaining, political choices are made that lead transitions in particular directions, not necessarily out of high regard for one regime type over another, but because the regime opted for is the most logical one given the circumstances of the political environment and the elites involved in the negotiation process. If democracy is opted for, the masses will need to be brought along. In short, we argue that authoritarians opt for democracy because they see that no other alternatives exist but democracy. Is this really how countries become democratic? Is democracy morally superior, or at the very least, does some sort of common understanding about democracy exist that leads authoritarians to accept democracy? We downplay the significance of democracy as a choice when we describe its acceptance by authoritarian leaders as simply their realizing that no other viable alternatives exist. What about the nonauthoritarian elites who push the democratic dream? Are they mainly interested in democracy because no other alternatives exist?

Philosophers have considered the question of a best regime for several thousand years. They have come up with many reasons why, in theory, democracy is not the best regime. Usually this exercise brings philosophers who favor democracy back to arguing for democracy from the standpoint that it is the best regime *in practice* because the best nondemocratic regimes seem to be unobtainable or useful mainly for purposes of comparison. Authoritarians who make a democratic compromise may not agree that democracy is the best regime in theory or in practice, but many authoritarians have come to the conclusion that there is something about democratic ideals that are difficult to refute. The focus on bargaining among political elites engaged in democratic transitions is important. There is surely something more than dealmaking— more than acknowledging that no other viable alternatives to democracy exist. There must be something compelling about our choice that tells us why the alternatives are really no longer viable choices. What were the underlying ideals that leaders in the opposition and within the authoritarian regime fought for? What is the philosophical foundation of their ideas? Is the message they give the people believable or is it merely words that flatter or intimidate in order to gain support for their own sakes? Do they provide a moral vision for people to follow? Do they understand democratic philosophy? Do they pay much attention to rights or mostly elections? In what way has religion been used to support or oppose democracy? Which cultural attributes support democracy and which ones create barriers to democracy? Has the transition process transformed leaders and the people as democratic tenets begin to be practiced? In what ways do nonelites endorse democracy, strengthen democratic institutions, and give energy to democratic reforms? We are improving at addressing these issues, but we can do better.

In focusing on conflict among elites we have overlooked much of what makes democracy unique. When we begin to explain democratic transitions as a multifaceted phenomenon, we return to the heart of political science in addressing the hopes, desires, and passions of human beings. Authoritarians find it difficult to convince others that a nondemocratic regime is the best regime because it fails to acknowledge the larger potential of individuals, their rights, their belief in justice, and their ideas about right and wrong. There is real intellectual power that drives the democratization process. It is not merely a struggle elites engage in over a period of time that eventually results in a democratic compromise. Because we have overlooked the guts of democratic promise, we have only been successful in describing the outward aspects of democratic transitions. A good study on democratic transition must include attempts to determine the relationship of new-found democratic freedoms to the religious, cultural, and familial traditions of countries that lend to or detract from democratic ideals. It leads us to consider institutions like schools, private associations, and economic institutions to determine how far the democratic ethic has taken root in societies. In this regard, democratization involves far more than bringing the masses along; it assumes a vision of democracy is shared in common. If the transition has made a positive impact in most or all of these areas, it is more likely that democratic gains will be consolidated and a democratic spirit will take root. Democratic virtues are more likely to flourish and the possibilities of democracy enduring are greatly increased. Looking at transitions in this way breaks us away from the rigid focus on elite bargaining and elections that has characterized much of our study of democratic transitions.

Because we have reduced transitions to rational procedures, we have also tended to restrict our analyses in ways that limit our abilities even to explain processes as fully as we should. Modern social science has separated economics from politics and, in so doing, has overlooked the fact that liberalism is a philosophy that does not separate economics and politics because political freedom and economic freedom are driven by the same human desires. As Ronald Inglehart has shown, elements of liberal culture have overspread the globe.[59] Rights language is of common use in democratic and nondemocratic countries. Authoritarian governments have bent liberal political definitions, concepts, and ideals in their attempts to extend the longevity of their regimes; but this only demonstrates the power of liberal ideals. These ideals are very important in explaining why so many countries, even poor countries that have few of the cultural attributes that democratic countries have, opt for democracy. In other words, the lack of a few preconditions to democracy in this or that country does not mean that they have not been prepared for democratization. Because we are not always successful in finding direct connections between economic promise or cultural change and democratic transitions, we have been too willing to focus only on those elements of actual political procedure. In so doing, we risk giving importance to only the most obvious elements in democratic transitions and overlook those factors that can give us a much fuller picture of why countries democratize.

All of these considerations need a starting point. This means we must conceptualize democracy accurately. We need to use our definition of democracy introduced in the first chapter to assess the quality of regimes in transit to democracy. How fully has a philosophy of liberal rights been established and what sources of virtue are there that support these rights? How much do the justifications for democracy relate to our conceptualization of democracy? What has been done to enable the new regime to become like the ideal contained in our definition of democracy? These questions correspond closely to the concerns of democratic consolidation. We turn to this discussion in the next chapter.

3

Consolidating Democracy

Which factors seem to be most conducive to the consolidation of democracy? Initial elections borne out of struggle, compromise, and hope for a better life have been held, but consolidating democratic gains is not easy. Some countries are able to make great progress toward consolidation with a few early successes in spite of the fact that they might be facing incredible odds in the economic realm or in other key areas. Others have economic success on their side, stable borders, a literate population that wants to embrace democracy, but consolidation fails to occur. In this chapter we review what comparativists have learned about democratic consolidation. In the 1980s and 1990s many countries were in transition to democracy. Scholarship has since focused on how these countries are or are not consolidating democratic gains. We also offer a critique of consolidation theory and suggest some ideas of traditional political science that have been too readily discarded by modern social science, leaving us with only a partial picture of democratic consolidation. This chapter calls for us to look at democracy as it was defined in the first chapter—a regime built on democratic rights and virtues. This base of rights and virtues gives rise to a civil society, characterized by quality public and private institutions organized to facilitate and serve people's livelihoods, leisure interests, and religious devotion, and an ethic of democracy that builds citizen respect for democratic laws and provides parameters for how people behave and think about the political system in which they they live.

Two Democratizing Countries, Two Very Different Outcomes

It is useful to consider the experiences of countries that are struggling to consolidate their democratic gains. This will provide us examples that can illuminate the usefulness and shortcomings of our theoretical work on consolidation. Let us consider two countries that vary greatly in their individual experiences with democracy. Peru's democracy has been characterized by democratic gains and setbacks for much of the twentieth century. The democratic government in Taiwan is new, though it has had considerable success in consolidating democracy.

Peru: Democratic Elections but No Democracy

After a decade of democratic set backs, Peru is once again counted among the ranks of democratic countries. Alejandro Toledo was elected president in June 2001, succeeding Interim President Valentín Paniagua who took power in November 2000 after President Alberto Fujimori went into self-exile in Japan. Toledo's election marks a return to democracy after ten years of assault on Peru's democratic institutions by Fujimori, who dismantled the legislature, courts, and media institutions in the name of direct democracy. Indeed, Peru has been unable to consolidate democratic gains that began in 1975. Most critics blame Peru's failure to consolidate democracy in recent years on Fujimori, who took extra-constitutional measures that he incorporated into the constitution to maintain his dominant role in the government. To be sure, Fujimori was certainly not the first Peruvian leader to demonstrate an ambivalent attitude toward democracy. In this century, Peru has had several transitions to democracy where elections have been held; but they have also been plagued with political instability including six military coups between 1920 and 1980. The problem is that Peru's democratic strides have never led to democratic stability and the sense that democracy was "the only game in town." Instead presidents have often used their powers to intimidate critics in and out of government, and they have claimed special privileges that have weakened democratic resolve among other civilian and military leaders. Peru's top leaders have almost always represented a very narrow stratum of elites of European dissent. They did little to expand policies that would benefit the rest of the country, while authoritarians like Generals Manuel Odria and Juan Velasco did make attempts to address the economic concerns of rank-and-file Peruvians.[1]

Among the more notable attempts at democracy is the 1975 coup in which General Francisco Morales Bermúdez took power. He cleared the path for a return to civilian rule by holding a national election to choose delegates to an assembly charged with promulgating a constitution. The new constitution was completed in 1979 and afforded universal suffrage for adults, among other key constitutional guarantees of freedom. First elections for the president and Congress were held in 1980, and all political parties were allowed to participate.[2] Fernando Belaúnde Terry was elected president, and his party won an outright majority in congress. Burdened with inefficient national industries that strangled the economy, the president and Congress sought to liberalize Peru's economy in hopes of lessening poverty and inequality. However, the new government was plagued by a powerful insurgency group of Maoist terrorists known as the Sendero Luminoso or "Shining Path." Paying little attention to the civil authorities, the military took strong measures of their own to combat the terrorists; but their tactics were cruel and indiscriminate. Critics of the military called for human rights inquiries and safeguards against military excesses. Unable to make effective gains in the economy and against terrorism, Belaúnde's regime faltered. In 1985, Alan García Pérez was elected president. He promised to reverse Belaúnde's attempts to denationalize industries and pledged to root out the Shining Path and other insurgency groups.[3] Unfortunately, right-wing paramilitary groups and the military took stronger measures to shore up their power, and the civilian government was weakened even more.[4] By 1990, it appeared as though elections might be disrupted by the Shining Path, the Movimiento Revolucionario Tupac Amaru (MRTA), and other insurgency groups, or by the military. In spite of these threats, the elections proceeded, though the results clearly showed the country lacked a consensus on what should be done to combat the country's growing problems. A relatively unknown candidate, Alberto Fujimori, was elected president representing an independent coalition of parties. He pledged honesty and the use of new technologies to spark growth in the Peruvian economy. He promised economic growth without the kinds of drastic measures that had proven difficult for the people of Peru under previous administrations.

Shortly after his election, however, Fujimori abandoned key campaign promises and announced sweeping economic changes. His plan was to privatize the economy, sell off nationalized companies and industries, and end subsidies for food and other basic goods. While most economists outside of Peru hailed Fujimori's courageous plan, many Peruvians who lived on the edge found the measures extreme and saw their immediate economic conditions worsen with the sweeping reforms. Still, Fujimori's policies brought about changes that were good for the economy insofar as new banking rules were established and Peru's position changed for the better in the international economy. However, the reforms provoked increased opposition and domestic unrest. In November 1991, Fujimori took advantage of a 150-day emergency, legislative power decree given to him six months earlier and announced plans to introduce more economic reforms. He was widely criticized for taking such strong measures. Many critics called for Fujimori's ouster and claimed his actions were unconstitutional. Fujimori claimed that the extreme measures were not without foundation. He contended Congress was stalling economic progress in Peru and that in order to solve the country's problems, bold measures had to be taken to ensure a bright economic future for Peru.

The austere economic measures led to increased attacks by the Shining Path and other rebel groups. Opposition to Fujimori's policies began to grow. He brought Vladimiro Montesinos into his government to serve as a legal adviser. Montesinos was a former army captain convicted of selling Peruvian military secrets to the United States and a man with ties to illegal drug dealers. Under Fujimori, Montesinos headed Peru's secret service and coordinated efforts among the National Intelligence Service (SIN), the army, and the presidency to intimidate government leaders and members of the opposition who challenged Fujimori's plans. These efforts included kidnapping, assault, illegal arrest and detention, and even murder.[5] The Congress and the president increasingly found themselves at odds with each other. Finally, in 1992, complaining that Congress was unwilling to act responsibly to turn around Peru's problems and charging its members of corruption, Fujimori announced a new program to combat terrorism, drug trafficking, government corruption in the congress and judiciary, and a plan to complete privatization of the economy. He claimed to fear gridlock in Congress even though Fujimori had a clear majority in Congress who favored his policies. In hindsight, it is apparent that Fujimori and Montesinos feared the legislature and courts would object to the lawless activities of SIN and the army and wanted a free hand to rule as they pleased.[6] Fujimori handed down an interim set of laws to replace the 1979 constitution. It gave the president legislative power and allowed him to fashion the judiciary and other government organs in a manner that would create a more favorable environment for him to operate according to his desire. With the help of Montesinos, the military supported Fujimori's efforts, believing that his bloodless coup would bring order and stability to Peru. Troops occupied government buildings and media establishments. Broadcasting was limited to material approved by Fujimori and the military. Some leaders were placed under house arrest, some resigned, and others protested Fujimori's overthrow of democracy. While politicians, the courts, and the media objected to Fujimori's coup, his actions received broad public support. Casting aside their previous reservations, Peruvians believed Fujimori's tactics were the right tools at the right time. In fact, Fujimori's self-coup or *autogolpe* had the support of 80 percent of Peru's people.[7]

Fujimori made some attempts to address charges that he had abandoned democracy. He held elections in October 1992 to choose an interim constituent congress to oversee constitutional changes and to legitimize reforms that he wanted to see implemented. Opposition leaders and political parties had been so intimidated through the Montesinos machine, however, that Fujimori was able to hand-pick those who would gain power in the congress. Constitutional changes were completed in 1993 though Fujimori maintained much control over government ministries, the courts, and other important organs of power in the country. Presidential elections were held in April 1995, and Fujimori handily defeated Javier Pérez de Cuéllar (the UN secretary-general from 1982 to 1991). He also granted amnesty to military leaders accused of human rights violations in order to bolster his support within the military. In spite of the democratic elections for president, Peru's democracy was floundering. Many leaders in the Fujimori cabinet were corrupt. Fujimori remained popular, however, because of his arrest of the leader of the Shining Path and his crushing of the MRTA. The public applauded his ability to bring law and order to Peru in spite of systematic human rights violations and destruction of democratic institutions. There were other problems brewing, however. Fujimori's hold over the political system had all but destroyed Peru's already weak political parties. Candidates ran for office on the basis of their own political popularity rather than the endorsement of a political party or carefully articulated platform. This kept Fujimori's position secure as the electoral system fell into disarray. There were border problems with Ecuador that took attention away from the domestic abuses Fujimori had inflicted on Peru. Perhaps most serious of all, Fujimori's temptation to work beyond legal limits led to a pattern of constitutional abuse. He declared plans to run for a third term in the year 2000. This was made possible by declaring he was not bound by the two-term limitation in office because he was first elected president under the 1979 constitution, which contained no such limit. His selective interpretation of constitutional passages undermined the purpose of constitutional reforms. He managed through practice and by constitutional manipulation to strengthen the role of the president and weaken the legislature and other democratic organs.

In May 2000, an unidentified intelligence agent provided the media with a video tape clearly showing Vladimiro Montesinos giving an opposition candidate $15,000 to defect to Fujimori's alliance. This time Peruvians did not look the other way. As Fujimori was being sworn in for a third term, demonstrators marched in the streets of Lima. By November 2000, Fujimori had lost his support and fled to Japan. Montesinos disappeared and Valentín Paniagua took office as interim president and with a charge to prepare Peru for fair presidential and legislative elections and a return to democracy. Elected president in June 2001, Alejandro Toledo has difficult challenges ahead. Solution of Peru's problems requires broad participation from all sectors of the government. Even today, in spite of considerable economic growth, unemployment and underemployment remain high. The poverty rate remains at 54 percent of the total population.[8] Faith in democratic institutions will have to be rekindled as his taking office follows years of wire-taps, censorship of the media, illegal elections, gross neglect of the needs of women and children, and other human rights abuses at the hands of the military and police.[9] Fujimori increased Peru's anti-democratic climate and from time to time gained considerable public support along the way.[10] Despite the promise of the 1979 constitution, Peru remains a country where periodic democratic elections are held, but democratic consolidation remains unrealized. Toledo must strengthen democratic institutions and find ways for people to endorse democracy as the only acceptable form of governance. This will not be easy in a country that has lagged behind other Latin American countries in supporting democracy. Peru's people need basic economic reforms and to see their lives prosper. They need a democratic ethic to grow. As one observer put it:

> What do many Peruvians do when the traffic light is red? They look both ways and then go ahead. What do they do when there is a long line at the bank? They sneak in line, but then protest if someone else tries to do the same thing. If we cannot wait for the light to turn green, if we do not respect the people who have spent a longer time waiting in line, why should we be surprised to learn that a presidential adviser took advantage of his post and amassed a fortune in foreign bank accounts? It is just a

matter of scale. If education does not discourage this petty misbehavior, it will be very difficult to fight against serious political abuses. Everyone, and especially the young, must understand that each person's rights end exactly where those of others begin.[11]

A change in the way Peruvians view their political liberties and opportunities can help usher in a new regime—one where democracy does not end with a transition but consolidates and becomes the only viable regime.

Taiwan: A Textbook Case of Democratization

In stark contrast to Peru, things have gone quite well for Taiwan. Taiwan is officially recognized as a province of China by the government in Taipei and by the Chinese government in Beijing. Democratic developments on the island, however, have made Taiwan a de facto independent state.

Taiwan became the refuge for the Nationalist government of China in 1949. Defeated on the Chinese mainland, the Nationalist military and government under the direction of Chiang Kai-shek fled to Taiwan in hopes of one day returning to the mainland and reclaiming control over all of China. Chiang's Nationalist (Kuomintang or KMT) rule on Taiwan was disciplined and brutal. Political opponents were imprisoned, tortured, and in some cases killed. All political parties except the KMT were prohibited. Newspapers were limited in what they could say and how many pages they could print on a daily basis. The military was overseen by political commissars. Primary and secondary schools as well as institutions of higher learning were watched over by KMT officials who made sure the curriculum conformed to official party doctrine. Nearly all elements of the 1947 constitution that guaranteed freedoms common to most liberal democracies were suspended in favor of an emergency decree of martial law that remained in effect until the late 1980s.

In spite of these oppressive measures, the KMT made great strides in developing Taiwan. A successful land reform program brought land, education, and improved technologies to farmers. Government-run or government-sponsored industries were created to foster construction of basic infrastructure in order to modernize Taiwan's industries and economy. Specialized schooling and higher education were emphasized in order to raise generations of highly educated workers, managers, and leaders. Short of mainland-born leaders, Chiang Ching-kuo, son of the elder Chiang, encouraged his father to bring in Taiwan-born technocrats and experts, in spite of the elder Chiang's realization that many Taiwan-born Chinese resented the KMT's oppressive political rule and dream of restoring the mainland under KMT control. The inclusion of young Taiwanese experts into government and industry brought about calls for reform within the KMT itself. Eventually this would compliment socio-economic reforms that were sweeping Taiwan as a result of highly successful development strategies and attractive export policies.

By the time Chiang Ching-kuo agreed to allow opposition parties to form in the late 1980s, Taiwan was a modern state in nearly every way except for democratic development. With Chiang's death in 1989, President Lee Teng-hui, a native Taiwanese himself, continued to oversee democratic changes. Free elections were held in the legislature and at the local level. Results of the elections were respected regardless of which candidate or party won. Leaders were allowed to take office and criticize government policies and individual leaders. Laws designed to root out corruption were debated and passed. Quality-of-life issues became more important to politicians and the people of Taiwan than they had ever been before. The KMT's chief opposition party, the Democratic Progressive Party (DPP), was free to call for independence for Taiwan, even though this position provoked China's anger. The DPP, though embittered over the repressive measures the KMT used on party members during the days of martial law, came to accept the KMT as a legitimate political party. Rather than seeking their removal on grounds of past crimes committed, the DPP agreed the arena for political competition had to include norms in which liberal regimes operate—elections, debates, legislative processes, judicial review. The KMT believed it could rely on its powerful organization. They believed their candidates would continue to be successful even with open and fair elections.

Along with democratic developments in the legislature, Taiwan's people readily accepted and enjoyed their new-found freedoms. News organizations were free to report and print a wide variety of political viewpoints without fear of reprisal. Schools were free to work through curricular issues by open discussion without party representatives looking over their shoulders. Security agencies were reformed: Harassment, illegal detentions, beatings, and other repressive measures were no longer tolerated. The military bowed out of politics, realizing that involvement in the ongoing political affairs would threaten the well-being of Taiwan's people. Some industries were separated from the government or from KMT ownership. Government ministries began to break from their KMT tutelage and embrace new standards of public service and professionalism. However, as the first fully democratic elections for president neared, two important issues remained unresolved—the question of Taiwan's political identity and a growing problem with political corruption. Both present real challenges to Taiwan's democratic gains.

In some countries about to elect a chief executive for the first time, there is fear that if defeated, the incumbent who has been a member of the former authoritarian regime may refuse to step down. There was little fear of this happening, primarily because Lee Teng-hui was quite popular and because democracy had progressed far enough that it was accepted by every significant constituency as the only viable political option for Taiwan. But Taiwan's democratization worried the Chinese immensely. There were real worries that all of Taiwan's newfound democratic freedoms could encourage Beijing to make good on its promise to attack Taiwan. After all, a democratic election for the president of Taiwan is in some respects a de facto pronouncement by the people of Taiwan for self-determination. Not only could they vote for president, but they were also free to vote for a candidate that openly advocated independence from China.

Reason prevailed in the presidential elections in spite of Beijing's attempts to intimidate Taiwan voters. For the most part, presidential candidates decided to leave Taiwan's status as is, neither an independent nation-state, nor an entity that bows to China's demands. Shortly before presidential elections were held, China conducted war games as a sign of protest over the elections. This served mainly to strengthen Taiwan's resolve to forge ahead with democracy. Lee Teng-hui won handily, and Taiwan continued its uneasy status as a democratic country that is officially a part of China. Because of this unique status, Taiwan lacks diplomatic representation in the United Nations and has few official government ties with other states. Despite this, Taiwan's democracy generates support from countries like the United States in unofficial ways.

A second threat to Taiwan's democratic gains is a large problem with corruption. As the reins of KMT leadership passed from the hands of a few born on China's mainland to many native-born Taiwanese, large numbers of local leaders engaged in graft. Projects were promised to particular constituencies in exchange for votes and financial support. Kickbacks are commonplace among Taiwan's political leaders. Fortunes have been amassed by businessmen who have lavished gifts and bribes on elected representatives. Money is in turn given to local constituencies to favor one candidate over others or to buy influence for the support of particular pieces of legislation. Investigations into corruption in Taiwan have revealed that the problem is so bad that scores of nationally elected leaders, and in some regions all local leaders, have been involved in illegal campaign activities.[12] The problem of corruption threatens democratic gains in a most basic way because it undermines the effectiveness of the democratic process. It also raises the question of whether Taiwan's people will continue to believe that democracy is morally superior to the repressive regime of the past that was able to keep graft under control.[13]

Still, Taiwan has made progress in convicting corrupt politicians, and popular sentiment has turned against dirty political practices. Corruption has become a dominant theme in Taiwan political debates and is considered a law-and-order question. The result has been greater oversight, improved methods of deterring and stopping graft, and penalties for offenders. In March 2000 the second freely contested presidential election resulted in the defeat of the KMT candidate because of questions over party corruption and the candidate's relationship to those tied to graft. Chen Shui-bian, the DPP candidate elected president, has pushed for reform at a pace that is acceptable to both elected officials and the citizens of Taiwan. Much more progress is needed to curb corruption, and the steps he is taking reinstill faith in democracy and open the door for further reforms down the road. The December 2001 legislative elections resulted in the ouster of the KMT as the majority party and put a coalition of parties, headed by the DPP, at the head of the legislature. The election marks a significant turning point for Taiwan as the country will now be led by politicians who favor Taiwan's independence from China.

Beyond elections, Taiwan's democracy has continued to meet new challenges. Procedural constitutional issues remain regarding the status of some representative bodies that have limited power or powers that are similar to existing and more efficient bodies. Taiwan has both a prime minister and a president, and the president enjoys dominant executive power. But the existence of two executives complicates matters in the legislature, especially since the president can appoint the prime minister without the legislature's approval. This has proved to be a major problem for President Chen in finding a prime minister with whom both he and the legislature can work. Most scholars agree the presidency is too powerful and needs to return some power to the legislature. This problem has become more acute given Chen's election. All of these issues mask the overriding problem of Taiwan's political identity. Will it continue to be a province of China in the future or can it gain official independence from China? The answer to this question is in large part dependent on

China's political and military development. For now, most people on Taiwan are willing to live with the island's ambiguous status.

Taiwan's relatively smooth transition from authoritarianism to democracy has no doubt improved the chances for a smooth consolidation process. In fact, many of the characteristics attributed to the consolidation process occurred in the transition process. It is unlikely that a country will have a transition to democracy completely bereft of the attributes important to consolidation. On this point it is interesting to note the different paths Taiwan and Peru have taken. Taiwan's economy has been a boon to democracy, whereas Peru's economy has weakened the efforts of democratic leaders. Peru's border problems with Ecuador and domestic insurgency led to a strengthening of the military, increasing its already powerful influence in Lima. Beijing's threats against Taiwan have in some respects strengthened democratic resolve. In addition, Taiwan's military has stayed clear of politics and has become a servant of the civilian government. Government policies in Taiwan are considered effective, and there is a proven record of accomplishment. Policies in Peru have a mixed record and a general sense of pessimism abounds regarding government reforms. Once political parties were allowed to organize in Taiwan, the government has not attempted to outlaw them or take unusual steps to control their influence. By contrast, Peru's weak political parties have been the targets of the government and military, and Fujimori kept parties from competing in a fair fashion. Fujimori was successful in struggling against formidable domestic challenges from the Shining Path and MRTA. Since the early 1950s, Taiwan has enjoyed relative high levels of domestic tranquility. The people of Peru have ambivalent feelings about democracy, while the people of Taiwan are ardent defenders of their democratic way of life.[14] These and other features underscore the variety of challenges regimes face when they try to consolidate democratic gains. Let us now turn to some of the scholarship on democratic consolidation in order to illuminate the different experiences of Taiwan and Peru as a way of assessing the strength and weaknesses of consolidation literature.

Scholarship on Consolidation

Some Early Efforts at Understanding Consolidation

The idea of democratic consolidation has been around for a very long time. The term democratic consolidation, however, is a relatively new one. Prior to using the term consolidation, comparativists referred to consolidated regimes as stable, mature, or successful democracies. Hence, we knew a consolidated regime (without using that term) was one that was not in danger of immediate collapse and that such a regime was characterized by a popular consensus that democracy was the best way of governance and that it performed well. Montesquieu, Tocqueville, and many of the American founders, as well as rank-and-file American citizens, believed democratic stability had much to do with virtue (a topic that we will deal with in detail in Chapters 4 and 5). This book concurs with this assessment. Democratic virtues play a key role in the establishment of political rights and in building civil societies. But political scientists in the post–World War II era have recognized the differences between democracies that were successful and those that were not, though not all have paid equal attention to democratic virtues.

Schumpeter identified five points he believed distinguished successful democracies from democracies that are in peril of collapse. His concern, however, was less on virtue and more on constitutional checks and balances and government performance:

1. Schumpeter pointed to the importance of quality leadership. Leaders must be willing and able to compromise on less important issues and persuade on important ones. There must be a process that cultivates good leadership for citizens of democracies.
2. Limitations on the range of decisionmaking powers need to be set. Politicians in democratic societies must not be allowed to go so far as to make sweeping changes that would in some way short-cut the democratic process. Decisions must be made with broad-based input and determined on the basis of what democracy can or cannot accommodate.
3. Democratic leaders need to rely on sound bureaucracies. Bureaucrats need to take pride in the civil service and work as partners with elected leaders in improving the quality of life in a democracy.
4. There must be agreement that laws passed by elected leaders are legally binding, that no group has the authority to selectively interpret laws or choose not to obey laws that have been passed under the mantle of democratic representation.
5. Finally, Schumpeter does suggest one virtue to be vital to democracy. Tolerance is essential to ensure respect for divergent

opinions. Tolerance would encourage discussion, debate, and compromise and would avoid ultimatums that undermine the sense of fair play that ought to exist in democracies.[15]

If we apply Schumpeter's criteria to our case studies, we see that Taiwan has benefited from leaders who have been willing to make compromises on matters that have cleared the way for the maintenance of democracy. Major political crises have been averted by seeking common ground on constitutional matters, though this balance could be interrupted by disagreements over the competing roles played by the president and prime minister. In the case of Peru, Fujimori considered compromise to be detrimental to his policies and either removed critics from office or neutralized their power by clandestine means. Early efforts by Interim President Paniagua and President Toledo demonstrate promise, but only the passing of time will reveal the quality of democratic leadership. Some doubt Toledo's ability to provide a vision for others to follow and criticize his reticence to deal with difficult issues facing the country. This promotes the prospects of petty political fighting rather than substantive decisionmaking and policymaking.

Taiwan's leaders have sought to strengthen the various branches of government and the bureaucracies. This has resulted in a stronger role for the legislature and judiciary than existed at the time of the transition to democracy. Peru has been harmed by executive organs that undermined the legislature and unduly influenced the courts. Bureaucracies were dominated by decrees rather than laws passed by congress, and some administrative bureaus served Fujimori and his appointees directly rather than Peruvians. Laws were seldom passed in Peru by legitimate procedure. Fujimori exercised ultimate authority over the law-making process. Bureaucracies want to be seen as professional and competent agencies, but they are limited in their abilities to serve because of no clear consensus between the president and congress on setting priorities for action. In Taiwan, the legislature and the president have found it necessary to work together to pass laws, though concern still exists over the strength of the executive vis-à-vis the legislature. There is no doubt the strength of the presidency benefited the KMT when their president was in power; but once a DPP candidate was elected, the KMT threatened impeachment for tactics President Chen used that were used by his KMT predecessor. Now that a DPP-led coalition leads the legislature, it will be interesting to see how Chen and the legislature will use their newfound powers. Finally, over the last decade or so, Taiwan has been very tolerant of divergent political opinions. Under Fujimori, media intimidation, human rights abuses, wire taps, and other authoritarian tactics were widely practiced to suppress speech in Peru. On the other hand, there is something of a tradition of toleration of competing political ideologies in Peru. In some regards, there are so many divergent political views in Peru that Peruvian politics has really lacked a political center —something that has not changed with the election of President Toledo. Because there is no real political center, political debate is in some regards rather ineffective.

By Schumpeter's criteria, Taiwan appears to have made significant progress in consolidating democratic gains while Peru has yet to consolidate. Other scholars believe these criteria are the product of more basic components of consolidation rather than the causes of consolidation. Lipset believes a key to democratic stability rested with political parties that had the support of significant segments of the population. These parties have to represent "multiple group identities" across racial, ethnic, religious, and economic lines. A vibrant party system provides the litmus test of democracy. For Lipset this test essentially confirms that a democracy without a significant political movement opposed to political parties who go by the democratic rules of the game is a quality democracy.[16] In light of this argument, Taiwan has embraced a multi-party system, whereas the party system in Peru has been seriously damaged. Prior to Fujimori's election to the presidency, Peruvian political parties competed without interference, though historically party organization has been weak in Peru. In this regard, Lipset's focus on parties does not explain the complexity of the Peruvian case as well as Schumpeter's criteria does. Almond and Verba have argued that an essential element of a successful democracy is the existence of governing elites who are able to build a civic culture that fosters democratic stability.[17] Their assertion does not tell us much about what consolidation is, but it does tell us that elites play a key role in consolidating a democratic regime. Dahl suggests polyarchies are never fully democratized but are regimes that are "substantially popularized and liberalized, that is, highly inclusive and extensively open to public contestation."[18] An inclusive state that is open to contestation does not guarantee stability but is nevertheless indicative of a mature polyarchy. Again, both Taiwanese and Peruvian elections have been open to public contestation, but one hesitates to proclaim either country's democracy consolidated.

To be sure, both the transition and consolidation phases of democracy are dependent on good leadership (as pointed out by Schumpeter, Lipset, Almond, and Verba) and the acceptance of some rules such as a willingness to bargain, compromise, and debate. In addition, effective government bureaucracies have always been acknowledged as being important. If we were to apply what these scholars have suggested above, we might assume that Taiwan has had better leadership than Peru, that the bureaucracy has worked well with elected leaders in Taiwan and not as well in Peru, and that there is more agreement on limits to power in Taiwan than in Peru. We could even sketch out a study showing this to be the case. While all of these ideas are important and relevant to our discussion, it is important to note than none of these studies tells us much about how consolidation occurs. Explanatory power is severely limited because early comparative studies made no effort to study transitions and consolidation phases separately. In some respects this is understandable. Very often the reasons why regimes do not complete transitions are the same reasons why they do not consolidate. As stated earlier, the factors involved in successful transitions have a direct bearing on the prospects for success in consolidating democratic gains. Even though democratization is a continual process from authoritarianism to democratic maturity, we have to separate the study of democratic development into phases. Without separating the phases, we immediately encounter problems in trying to understand why democracy is working in Taiwan but is still struggling to survive in Peru. Our studies of the last decade have made it easier to study transitions from authoritarianism as one phenomenon and the consolidation of democracy as another. They have improved the quality of our scholarship and have given us greater explanatory power. How did this theoretical breakthrough occur?

As comparativists' disillusionment grew during the 1970s over democracy's prospects in the developing world, some studies emerged that analyzed reasons for the collapse of democracy. In their work on the breakdown of democratic regimes, Linz and Stepan called for a return to studying democratization, this time looking at the transition from authoritarianism to democracy as one focal point and the study of democratic consolidation as a separate focal point.[19] This call for greater attention to the overall democratization process resulted in the seminal *Transitions from Authoritarian Rule* study edited by O'Donnell, Schmitter, and Whitehead, as well as other important works on democratic transitions. As the third wave of democracy progressed, scholars found it increasingly important to understand the processes behind consolidation, as some transitions from authoritarianism had already reverted to authoritarianism in part or in whole without scholars adequately able to explain why the regimes had been able to consolidate.[20] Hence studies in the late 1980s and early 1990s tend to focus on transitions to democracy, while work from the mid- to late 1990s has emphasized consolidation. While this new scholarship has not completely replaced earlier work on consolidation, it is more useful because it has studied the consolidation process separately from transitions. This has allowed for more detailed analysis and careful attention to specific cases where consolidation has and has not been successful. The result has been a much larger body of theory with better applicability to a variety of countries' experiences.

Recent Work on Consolidation

Significant debate still exists concerning what democratic consolidation actually is. This is not merely a difference of opinion concerning words and definitions. There are fundamental differences at the root of the debate. As noted above, early conceptions of democratic consolidation tended to focus on the idea that a democracy is consolidated if it is stable. There are two reasons for accepting a minimalist definition such as this. The first is that a simple definition of consolidation sets the concerns of well-established democracies aside from the immediate concerns of newly democratized countries. Democracies can be consolidated but still lack the quality or the complexity of democracies that have been in existence for some time. A second reason to accept a minimalist definition is that it tends to focus on the institutionalization of a single defining element—usually elections, and little else. Some scholars believe that a basic criterion of democracy—ongoing democratic elections—should be our primary concern while other issues concerning institutional development, civil and political society, and the like are free to develop according to the political culture of any given country and are not bound by a standard common to Western Europe or North America. This is essentially the argument of Adam Prezworski and associates.[21] But prior to democratization, the KMT allowed local races to be fairly contested while they sharply limited contests for national posts. Similarly, elections in Peru worked well in replacing leaders until Fujimori changed the rules. The problem arises, if not elections as a determinant of consolidation, then what? Guillermo O'Donnell has warned us that by using more ambitious criteria of defining consolidation, we may preclude the possibility of accepting informal institutional ways of conducting the business of a democratic society that may emerge in various countries.[22] He cautions us not to become too ambitious in our approach and not to set criteria that have little or nothing to do with democratic experience. For this reason, elections, he argues, are the most important element of democratic consolidation. In recent work, however, O'Donnell has modified his position. He believes elections are not the only criterion that can be used to evaluate consolidation. If elections are institutionalized (meaning they occur at regular intervals and are respected by political contestants and citizens), and meet other minimal qualifications (such as a legal system that backs individual rights that are inalienable), we come closer to realizing a universal definition of democracy that transcends cultural boundaries.[23]

There are many who agree with Prezworski in using elections as the primary determinant of a consolidated regime. They hold that although it is a minimalist definition, it remains useful because methodologically it contains fewer assumptions about what consolidation means and enables scholars to use a common language to talk about consolidation. Rather than mixing uses, definitions, and philosophical preferences about consolidation, others suggest we need to use more care in classifying types of democratic regimes. If we stick with the minimalist definition, and use greater care in identifying the attributes of specific democracies, we can avoid miscommunicating standards that limit our abilities to identify consolidated democracies.[24]

Some scholars accept aspects of the minimalist definition of democracy as far as testing whether or not a democracy is consolidated. As noted in the previous chapter, Samuel Huntington has proposed the "two-turnover" test to determine if incumbents will willingly leave office after losing elections. But critics of the minimalist definition of consolidation argue that elections are but a single aspect of democracy that overlooks the guts of democracy. Countries like Peru, for example, hold regular elections but do not always enjoy complete freedom of the press and freedom of speech. Legitimate complaints about the government have resulted in illegal detention and even torture for government critics. The military has retained domains of power independent of the civilian government. The elections themselves, though operative, were unduly influenced by President Fujimori, thus calling into question just how free they were. A more dependable test is desirable. Some have suggested that it would be useful to consider major challenges to democracy, such as coup attempts or other acts of political violence, to test whether or not a regime is consolidated.[25] By this criteria Peru would be disqualified as a consolidated democratic regime due to Fujimori's *autogolpe*. But it is pointed out that drastic events may not be reliable determinants of democratic consolidation. Actions such as coups, assassinations, and social unrest can challenge the staying power of democracies that have been consolidated for some time. In the early days of his administration, President Franklin Roosevelt worried what effect the political demonstrations of World War I veterans were having on the mood of the country. He believed that social unrest in Washington, coupled with the country's economic problems in general, had the potential of wreaking havoc on American democratic institutions. Some militia groups oppose the democratic government of the United States and have even committed violent acts, but nobody questions whether or not the United States is a consolidated democracy. Most scholars, to a greater or lesser degree, agree that unusual or severe tests such as these do not necessarily reflect regime consolidation. Instead, some argue we should consider the public statements of leaders in government, political parties, spokespersons in social movements, and other public pronouncements, documents, and symbolic gestures that seem to suggest democracy is the only legitimate way to power.[26] It is this broad-based consensus about democracy and the resolve of all major actors to see democracy succeed that have led to consolidation in Taiwan. As democratic reforms were instituted, faith in democracy grew. Democratic reforms in government led to democratic norms being adopted in all sorts of public settings including the KMT, which in its authoritarian days had a Leninist organization. The transformation of the KMT as a democratic party has indeed been a very public symbol of democratic sentiment in Taiwan. Because of similar experiences in other democratizing countries, scholars have come to accept a wider interpretation of consolidation than focusing on elections.

There are probably no students of democratization who doubt the importance of institutionalized elections. But most believe that certain principles must be honored in order to truly declare a democracy consolidated. Recent interest has focused on matters of civic life and political culture in relation to democratic consolidation. Larry Diamond has suggested that the emergence of a civil society is essential for consolidation to occur. Although elites and democratic leadership matters, Diamond argues we need to look at civil society much in the same way Tocqueville did in his study of America—by looking at its various civic institutions. According to Diamond, civic institutions, be they economic, educational, informational, or interest-based, perform important functions leading to consolidation that cannot be met in other ways. Civic institutions limit state power, supplement political authority, encourage tolerance and moderation, create opportunities for interest articulation, foster cross-cultural dialogue and problem solving, recruit and train civic leaders, disseminate information, and enhance government accountability and evaluation of policies.[27] For Diamond, good leaders may be able to solve initial political problems, but until civic institutions exist and play the role described above, consolidation has not occurred. Other studies support this view. While comparativists used to think of consolidation in terms of regime survival, scholars have become increasingly aware that questions of survivability are directly linked with issues of democratic quality. Hence consolidated democracies are characterized by autonomous civil and political societies guaranteed by rule of law.[28] It is precisely this level of democratic development that was thwarted in Peru by domestic insurrection and authoritarian privileges claimed by President Fujimori. Independent civil and political institutions require a spirit of fair play, especially by key players in society. Fujimori's short-cutting of democratic procedure reintroduced authoritarian elements and prevented democracy from having a chance to reemerge and consolidate. Political disaffection became widespread in Peru. Despite his initial popularity, Fujimori became hated for his inability to solve Peru's deepest economic and political problems. By destroying civic institutions and preventing their development, Fujimori removed any hope that a democratic ethic would emerge as long as he continued to rule Peru. By contrast, the weaknesses of Taiwan's political institutions and corrupt leaders became the target of civil society. Educators, the media, industrial and financial leaders, religious leaders, and private organizations criticized the corruptive influences in government and pointed to weaknesses in the constitution that have contributed to the imbalance of power that favors the presidency over the legislature. Government leaders have felt it necessary to respond to the public's complaints by prosecuting corrupt leaders and pledging to reexamine government structure to better ensure government accountability and limitations on power. Critics inside the government could not have been effective in pointing out these problems on their own. It required the emergence of a civic-minded society.

Diamond's defense of civic institutions stands in contrast to arguments forwarded by some scholars who have suggested that civic cultures are a result of consolidation and not something that leads to consolidation.[29] They acknowledge that the requisites to democracy literature of the 1960s were correct in assuming that political culture is important to democracy—though such cultures are by and large a product of democratic consolidation and not necessarily a factor that leads to either democratic transition or consolidation. But Taiwan's presidential elections came after significant progress had been made to consolidate the regime. No significant leaders in Taiwan, in or out of government, had reason to believe elections would be unfair because leaders and voters had come to view the process as routine and healthy. Taiwan's experience is not alone in this regard. Democracies have a much greater chance of consolidating if a civic ethic has been nurtured during the transitional phase of democratization.

There are others who disagree with both explanations of when civil society and consolidation emerge. A growing number of analysts see simultaneous development of a civic culture alongside general cultural change. Ronald Inglehart, for example, suggests culture change is an intergenerational process in which the economy, politics, religious opinion, and culture in general undergo change together in coherent, and in some cases, predictable patterns. He argues these changes make some scenarios of social change more probable than others. Even though modernization is not linear, Inglehart believes there is a global trend toward socioeconomic change and democracy that is complementary.[30] Modern cultures tend to be democratic, capitalist, less reliant on religion, and share more in common with one another because they have rejected traditional ways that vary greatly from modern norms. The democratization experiences of countries in Southern Europe tend to support this thesis. As economic, political, and social development occurs across the board, development tends to be more consistent, which helps consolidate these democracies. Traditional attitudes have a direct influence on institutional development and threaten to slow the pace of democratic transition and consolidation.[31] The importance of transgenerational cultural changes is apparent in the cases of both Peru and Taiwan. Peru had a weak democratic legacy long before Taiwan had any experience with democracy. The influence of Catholicism in Peru has been a boon in this regard. Taiwan's tradition of unquestioned support for political authority resulted in a more gradual move toward democracy. But social, educational, and economic reforms were begun in the early 1950s in Taiwan, which greatly contributed to Taiwan's political development. In contrast, Peru's lack of success in implementing and maintaining meaningful socioeconomic reforms has hampered its abilities to build institutions and public attitudes that consolidate democratic advances.[32] In addition, though Catholicism cleared the way for the establishment of democratic ideals, the role of significant Catholic leaders in Peru has been seen by some as a barrier to democracy. The close relationship between the cardinal in Lima and President Fujimori led some to believe the church had not played as significant a role in democratic reform as it could. In addition, some scholars see little effort on the part of the church to teach democratic virtues in Peru.[33]

But many comparativists resist the argument forwarded by Inglehart because they deem it too dependent on socioeconomic change without showing the impact of political ideas on social institutions.[34] They also claim he overlooks the key role played by elites. Though they have different theoretical perspectives that divide them, scholars like O'Donnell, Diamond, Linz, Stepan, and others believe that democratic attitudes penetrate other social spheres, be they economic or cultural, which in turn makes our primary social institutions take on a democratic character.[35] Such is the argument of Tocqueville and other philosophers who have considered the question of democratization. The spirit of democracy is infectious. Successful democratic ideas generate popular support for democracy. Hence, civil and political institutions and democratic laws have become the defining elements of democratic consolidation. In the recent scholarship, these principles are perhaps best summarized by the work of Linz and Stepan, who believe that consolidated regimes contain behavioral, attitudinal, and constitutional aspects that set them apart from democracies that have not been able to move beyond the transitional phase of democratic elections.

1. Behaviorally, a democratic regime is consolidated if no significant actors attempt to secede from the state or create a nondemocratic alternative to the democratic state. Peru did not qualify as a consolidated state behaviorally because President Fujimori thwarted democracy and the military continued to reserve its own domain of power. It is unclear whether Fujimori was ever a believer in democracy as much as he was a believer in his own abilities to lead Peru. If you believe other goals to be

more important than democracy, then democratic rules are going to be far less important than other rules put to use. Taiwan's leaders are more clearly behaviorally inclined toward democracy, though the constitutional imbalance that favors the executive branch of government indicates a corrective is in order. At any rate, a democratic consensus must build in Peru, as it has done in Taiwan, before we can be sure that the behaviors of significant actors are compatible with democratic governance.

2. Attitudinally, a democratic regime is consolidated when a significant majority of the public believes that democracy is the best regime and hence the best way to govern a society. Peru has failed to consolidate attitudinally because Peruvian leaders have not done enough to nurture enthusiasm for democracy among the people. Democracy lacks a track record of providing Peruvians with meaningful socioeconomic and democratic reforms. As a result, Peru lacks a democratic ethic in civil society. Many Peruvians hold the same suspicions of democratic rules that leaders like Fujimori held. Taiwan has had considerable success consolidating attitudinally. The democratic ethic has penetrated more than formal political institutions. Democratic ways have led to the development of all kinds of private institutions and have liberalized the ways existing organizations govern themselves. Democratic rights are expected, and people savor their newfound political freedoms. Would this remain true in the event mainland China's threats to take Taiwan by force become more imminent? Perhaps the people of Taiwan or any democratic republic would consider such a test to be too great of a deterrent to consolidation. But so far, China's threats have strengthened the democratic resolve of Taiwan's people.

3. Constitutionally, a democratic regime is consolidated when all forces, governmental and nongovernmental, become subject to and habitualized in dealing with conflict within legal parameters established by the democratic regime.[36] While both countries have struggled in this regard, Taiwan has had considerable success of staying within the limits of the constitution. But with the election of Chen Shui-bian, the redundancy of having two chief executives and the strength of the presidency are matters that need immediate attention. This is perhaps the greatest threat to Taiwan's democracy. Peru's constitution was picked apart and rewritten at the whim of President Fujimori. He did this outside legal boundaries, which increased skepticism about the prospects for respecting the rule of law in Peru. Lima needs leaders who will follow constitutional procedure and champion the democratic elements contained in the constitution.

The above three points speak to consolidation as a phenomenon that contains principles that go far beyond mere elections. They speak to the existence of a civil society akin to the notion of civil society common to the established Western democracies of North America and West Europe. A consolidated democracy is free of authoritarian thinking and the trappings of authoritarianism. It is an acknowledgement that democracy is the only acceptable regime. Civil life operates autonomously, and the economic sector is free to operate without government interference. Indeed, all kinds of institutions—religious, interest-based, civic, and economic—function freely. To a great extent, civil life enables citizens to create their own rules of conduct and to act as the conscience of democratic society. In a consolidated society, civil and political societies merge, and citizens find they have multiple interests and identities, be they ethnic, religious, economic, political, or interest-based. And because political society must answer the demands of civil society and provide political policy, it establishes constitutional limits to both empower and limit government in a democratic society. Laws come to embody democratic philosophy and provide a template for acceptable democratic behavior in addition to legitimizing government through administrative rules and responsibilities.[37] Political institutions like political parties, representative bodies, electoral processes, and government ministries are respected. Liberal freedoms based on political rights for all people are constitutionally guaranteed.[38] By this standard, we see the real strength of Taiwan compared to Peru. A vibrant civil society has emerged in Taiwan, and the method of measuring government performance and quality of private life in Taiwan is by democratic criteria. Sadly, civil society in Peru is poorly developed. People still look to government for answers to most of their problems without being able to build and rely upon institutions of their own making to improve life in Peru. This presents President Toledo with a formidable task—to develop democracy in Peru behaviorally, attitudinally, and constitutionally in hopes of building not only a democratic government, but also a civil society.

The differences between the definitions given by Linz and Stepan and Prezworski and others are readily apparent. To date, Linz and Stepan's understanding of consolidation has found widespread acceptance. It is notable that recent scholarship on consolidation focuses more on political attitudes, thinking about democracy, and the concerns of democratic political philosophy rather than simply the procedural functions of democracy. This is apparent from the criteria used above to define consolidation. It is a scholarly trend that is a vast improvement over earlier efforts to understand what lends to democratic stability because we consider more of what day-to-day life is like in a democratic regime rather than focusing on a single criterion like elections. There are philosophical and practical concerns that must be addressed in studying consolidation. Recent scholarship has given us ambitious criteria to meet, so we now ask the question: How does a democracy consolidate? What are the conditions, factors, and forces that have proven useful and dangerous in the process of consolidation?

The Path to Consolidation

Scholars recognize that consolidation does not often occur in an orderly fashion after the transition process but may occur simultaneously with the process of transition.[39] They also acknowledge that the conditions that brought about a transition from authoritarianism may also bring about consolidation or endanger the prospects for consolidation. Some countries experience contentious transitions but consolidate in a more orderly fashion. Indeed, every country's consolidation experience has unique attributes. Different actors, institutions, and circumstances play significant roles at various times in the democratization process. And the time it takes a regime to consolidate varies. Even though a country may have consolidated, consolidation does not guarantee long-term democratic success.[40] Circumstances that may bring down a consolidated democracy in one country may have little or no effect on another. Some countries may be able to consolidate democratic gains but then struggle to deepen democracy.[41] Although Greece is a consolidated country, high levels of corruption have had a detrimental impact, and Greece's ability to acquire the level of democratic quality that is enjoyed by other countries has been limited. The same can be said of Taiwan. Democratic gains are beginning to be consolidated, but political corruption has the potential of leading to instability and public displeasure with democracy. Voters in Taiwan have considered political corruption to be the most significant political problem, even more important than threats from mainland China. So far the people of Taiwan have relied on the courts to prosecute dishonest politicians and on elections to vote out leaders believed to be involved in graft. For now the people have faith in their electoral institutions and the courts; but anger over corruption can increase if other things are not going well. Peruvians were willing to overlook allegations of dishonesty within the Fujimori regime as long as groups like the Shining Path were being rooted out, and the economy showed signs of improving. As the economy struggled, however, Fujimori's popularity sagged. When Montesinos was implicated in bribery, the bubble burst for Fujimori, forcing him out of office. The burden now falls on President Toledo to rebuild confidence in democratic institutions and convince people that democratic rules will be honored by his administration. This is a formidable task because there is still doubt in Peru over whether democracy can deliver what the country needs.

A key to establishing a quality, consolidated democracy in large measure rests with the abilities and efforts of elites to establish civic virtues and constitutional rules. For this reason, most scholars focus on elite efforts in studying consolidation, just as they have in studying the process of democratic transitions. It is elite factions in government, business, trade unions, state agencies, and other public and private institutions that determine what kinds of agreements are to be made, what kinds of policies should prevail, and, in the long run, how democracy will be consolidated. If elites are caught in contentious political debates or cannot solve large social issues at the time of a democratic transition, these problems will almost certainly complicate efforts to consolidate democratic gains. Consider the huge difference of opinion among successive Peruvian presidents over whether or not to denationalize state-run industries. The on-again, off-again economic reforms have undermined faith in democracy. This created conditions where Fujimori could mastermind an *autogolpe* with popular approval because the people admired his resolve to fix the economy. Additionally, indigenous groups in Peru have not supported democracy. Democratic leaders' inability to crush these movements led to Fujimori's aggressive pursuit of these groups. His popularity soared with the crushing of the Shining Path and MRTA, even though the Peruvian army committed gross human rights violations along the way. These kinds of problems have the potential of raising doubts, not only in leaders' minds, but also in the minds of people living in countries with problems similar to Peru's.

Scholarship has shown that if those involved in the democratization process pay attention to several key areas, the chances of democratic consolidation can be enhanced. Some of these deserve special attention.

Reserve Domains of Power

A major impediment to democratic consolidation is the existence of reserve domains of power that seek to limit or reverse democratic gains.

These include military leaders who may oppose democracy or have reservations about the prospects of democracy. Monarchs or other authoritarians may want to hold on to their power. Other government leaders within representative or state institutions may have mixed feelings about democracy. Capitalists, religious leaders, or other nonstate actors may oppose policies of the emerging democratic regimes. In nearly all of these areas, Peru has suffered. The military has been jealous of its power and refused to submit to civil authority. This can be explained in part by the extraordinary threat posed to Peru from indigenous groups like the MRTA and the Shining Path. President Fujimori's authoritarian ways and his willingness to overlook human rights abuses at the hands of the military have also preserved the military's position as an obstacle to democracy. Through Montesinos, the military formed an alliance with SIN and the rest of Fujimori's inner circle that supplanted democratic procedures with a ruling clique. Studies have shown that the military's willingness to go along with democratic changes in Southern Europe was a huge factor in the development of democracy in that part of the world, while the continued involvement of the military in Latin American countries continues to create an impediment to democratic consolidation. Unless Latin American countries can continue to move civilian leaders into key positions currently held by military officers, the chances of consolidation wither.[42]

While reserve power domains have delayed Peru's prospects for lasting democracy, the absence of reserve domains of power has proven to be a boon for other countries. Taiwan has benefited by not having groups who retain significant power outside the legitimate circle of democratic contestation. As democracy took hold in Taiwan, a spirit of cooperation tended to douse the hottest fires of political extremism among government and opposition leaders alike. Some worried that Taiwan's bureaucrats would continue to prove loyal to several key political figures from Taiwan's authoritarian past. But the bureaucracy has been successful in building an image of professionalism and public service. They have severed inappropriate ties to the Nationalist Party and have pledged loyalty to the constitution.

Elite Skill and Democratic Success

If the attitudes of principle elites on all sides of the political equation are willing to move toward democratization, not only is the transition usu-

ally smoother, but also the course for consolidation may be smooth. In
the event that consolidation fails, and a breakdown of democracy is experienced, it is not impossible to rekindle fervor for democracy at a later
date. Such is the experience of many countries that democratized prior
to and immediately following World War II.[43] It is difficult for the same
leader to flounder back and forth between authoritarianism and democracy and still be seen as a serious defender of democratization. President Fujimori showed no resolve to democratize. In fact, he had gone
too far and suspended too many democratic institutions to have ever
been taken seriously as a democratic reformer. With his self-imposed
exile and exposure as a corrupt, self-absorbed authoritarian, Fujimori
created conditions that favored a democratic alternative. Interim President Paniagua and especially President Toledo have had to meet the
expectations of Peruvians who demand basic socioeconomic improvements and a return to democracy. The prospects of both happening simultaneously would be greatly enhanced if the leadership of the Senate
can also devote themselves to building democratic institutions and going by democratic rules. But in the months following Toledo's election,
pessimism has begun to be replace hope. Elites see Toledo's electoral
success to be as much a product of historical circumstance as personal
skill. Too many promises were made in the campaign that few if any
Peruvians believe can be met, and there is a widespread belief that Toledo lacks the political skill and power to accomplish significant tasks.

Elite and mass behavior in political negotiations during and after the
transition to democracy is important. If leaders on all sides seek moderation and are willing to manage social conflict through cooperation
and with a steady eye on the democratization process, consolidation is
more achievable. Once again, however, if the military or any other significant groups decide the costs of repression are less than the costs of
conceding a democratic compromise, consolidation may be seriously
undermined. Observers of the Taiwan transition and consolidation process wondered if democratic momentum would continue during negotiations in the late 1980s and early 1990s. Opposition leaders frequently
walked out of negotiation sessions, and KMT leaders often made unrea-
sonable requests that would have maintained political privilege and undermined democratic reforms. But opposition leaders plead their case
before moderate KMT figures and the media. KMT negotiators offered
compromises and the negotiations resumed. At no time did KMT or
DPP leaders threaten ultimatums that permanently blocked reform

progress. The quality of reforms has been somewhat compromised in regards to the constitutional powers of the executive. But at the time of the negotiating sessions, most leaders believed they should move on and try to deal with this problem at a later date rather than stalling reforms on a single issue.

Democratic Uncertainty and Political Memory

Memories of the preexisting authoritarian regime may help or hinder consolidation efforts. If the previous regime lacked success in policy implementation, it could bode well for the new regime that can benefit from effectively articulating and implementing policy. If the previous authoritarian regime was more successful at policy implementation than the new democratic regime, however, consolidation may be difficult to obtain as faith in democracy begins to fade. There was some reluctance on the part of Taiwan's people to move toward democracy. The economic success of the Kuomintang regime helped preserve their power, but it also caused many to wonder if economic success would continue in a democratic environment where policy consensus may not be possible. Elites in and out of government circles were able to win popular acceptance of democratic reforms through public discussion and encouragement. This helped ease people's minds in making the transition from an authoritarian regime that had done much economic good toward consolidating gains when democratic debate tended to become contentious. The failure and collapse of the Fujimori regime gave Toledo a boost at the polls, but as president he faces staggering challenges. Trouble with the economy or other domestic challenges out of his control could imperil his efforts. Popular dissatisfaction with democracy could build, or the military could attempt to reassert itself into Peruvian politics. None of these situations would be new to Peruvians, thus the importance of making significant democratic gains for Peru early in the Toledo administration is vital.

Keeping Expectations Under Control

If government officials can lower expectations of the people but reap success that is greater than promised, faith in democracy grows among both the leadership and the people.[44] This has proven to be a key point in understanding why democracy has succeeded in Southern Europe but lagged behind in Eastern Europe where economic expectations were too high for some new governments to satisfy. The same can be said for Peru. President Fujimori promised too much without fully informing Peruvians of the sacrifices that would be required to make the reforms work. The political costs of having sacrificed democracy for economic ends may not be apparent to many Peruvians, but democratic institutions have paid dearly. Toledo has also promised too much, though he seems convinced to follow a democratic path. Eventually, any economic plan will require broad-based government and private-sector cooperation rather than the president pushing through a handful of reforms by himself.

Political or economic haste raises the political stakes in any regime, especially a new democracy. Regimes that have experienced gradual transitions and consolidations have proven to be more successful in establishing viable democratic institutions than have regimes that have experienced rapid democratization.[45] Taiwan benefited greatly from steady development and reforms that introduced liberalization over the course of several decades. Peru's development has come in spurts and starts. Hence, no period of development can be looked upon by Peruvians as routine. They came to accept President Fujimori's cavalier disregard for democratic procedures as justified as long as the economy improved. In the long run, Fujimori failed to meet Peruvians' economic expectations. This puts added pressure on President Toledo to grow the economy and develop democratic institutions. If he is successful in deepening democracy and making significant economic gains, Peruvians could view economic and political failures as a product of authoritarianism.

Prioritizing Reforms

Newly established democratic regimes need to know where to focus their policy efforts. Huntington and others point out that it is very important for countries to have some level of economic development to bolster new democratic regimes. Economic development gives the new regime some time to develop policies that may have positive outcomes later. Usually the need for immediate economic success is not as great because the regime is not undermined by a lack of economic success early on.[46] But each country's experience will differ. Taiwan's economic development was seen as a boon to early efforts to democratize. Beginning in the 1950s, the government implemented an ambitious land-reform program that fundamentally changed the pattern of land tenancy.

The government emphasized education reforms and subsidized heavy industry. Infrastructure was developed through massive public works projects. All of these policies helped create Taiwan's "economic miracle," setting Taiwan on a path of development that became the envy of many governments in developing countries. Steady economic growth and gradual political reform led to distinct efforts to democratize by the 1980s. Democracy seemed a natural course to take because it complemented Taiwan's economic development and met the needs of a modern nation-state. All of these reforms gave leaders and the people of Taiwan confidence that they could weather some short-term political and economic uncertainty for the long-term benefits of democracy. This is a benefit Peru has not been able to enjoy. The absence of basic socioeconomic reforms and policies to ensure equal treatment and opportunities for all Peruvians has left the country deeply divided. Economic development is uneven. For decades Peruvians of European dissent had privileges the rest of the population did not enjoy. There is no natural democratic counterpart to Peru's level of socioeconomic development because too many glaring inequalities remain. President Toledo faces formidable challenges ahead. Should he emphasize structural economic changes first or political reforms? The early word from Peru is not so bright. Scholars explain Toledo has failed to promote a vision of economic or political reform. Without success in either the economy or government, democracy is imperiled.

Increasingly scholars suggest it is best for regimes to solve significant political problems first. Doing so can sometimes buy leaders time to deal more carefully with socioeconomic inequalities. Once socioeconomic inequalities are addressed (modest tax reforms and other immediate near-term social-welfare measures), only then should structural economic reforms (major income redistribution schemes, land reform, reorganization of financial institutions, etc.) demand the immediate attention of the new government. This proved to make a major difference in Southern Europe. Leaders in Spain and Portugal found it easier to develop political institutions prior to pushing for socioeconomic equality or introducing major economic reforms. In their democratization experiences, Southern European countries focused on political reforms first, social-welfare issues second, and structural economic problems last of all.[47] This contrasts with modernization theory, which suggests that economic reforms should be attempted first or at least simultaneously in order to give the new regime early successes. Scholars have found that citizens in consolidating countries are more sophisticated than perhaps previously thought in that they recognize that patience may be needed in waiting for economic improvements. They come to see that economic development is enhanced by democratization.[48] The people of Peru did not understand the problem of supporting Fujimori's antidemocratic ways. Because of the extraordinary problems with domestic unrest and the inability of past democratically elected presidents and members of Congress to build a consensus on economic reform, authoritarianism may have seemed logical, especially authoritarian attempts to reform the economy. But authoritarian economic policies often fall short of reaping the long-term economic benefits that come from a broad-based democratic approach to economic development.[49] The Taiwan case seems to contrast with the experiences of Southern Europe. Taiwan's economic reforms began long before, and indeed enjoyed much success prior to, democratization. But most third wave democracies that have been able to succeed in political reforms early on have had greater success in their efforts to reform the economy later.

Parliamentary Systems or Presidential Systems?

When constructing representative institutions, the general rule is that parliamentary systems are safer than presidential systems. The parliamentary systems of Southern Europe are viewed as a key factor that led to consolidation, whereas the tendency in South America to favor presidential systems has led to a subversion of democratic rules by overzealous presidents and challenges to executive power from the military and other challengers.[50] Dynamic parliaments are generally viewed as greater guarantees of democratic success because the parliamentary process requires prime ministers and members of parliament to work together to achieve legislative success.[51] Taiwan and Peru have both experienced difficulties by retaining presidential systems over parliamentary systems. Even though Taiwan does have a prime minister, the duties of that office are dwarfed by the president, who is the chief executive and elected separately from the legislature. Most scholars in Taiwan are in agreement that the office of the president maintains too much power vis-à-vis the legislature. In Peru the consequences of a strong president in relation to Congress are apparent. Fujimori has been able to operate the government relatively free of congressional interference. This resulted in constitutional reforms that strengthened the powers of the president.

In areas where the constitution does call for congressional involvement, Fujimori frequently chose not to observe the constitution. In spite of these abuses, there is widespread support for a presidential system in Peru because of the belief that strong leaders are needed to lead the country and bear responsibility for policy successes and failures. For now, there is no significant effort to replace the presidential system with a parliamentary system.

Constitution Making

Crafting an original constitution or making constitutional changes is very important work. Sometimes key players in the constitution-making process fight to retain privileges enjoyed by the previous authoritarian regime. Others may advocate the creation of a constitution that has symbolic importance but no practical significance. Sometimes constitutions are created by provisional governments that retain nondemocratic privileges or methods of conducting the affairs of state. In these cases, political power remains in the hands of a select group, and constitutional revisions fail to reform inept judicial institutions. All of these factors together or separately can weaken or destroy the constitutional foundation of a new democratic state. For consolidation to occur, it generally is held that the constitution-making process must employ as many key players as needed to ensure that the constitution will have the support of government leaders, civic organizations, and the general population.[52] Taiwan's experience in amending the constitution has been mixed. At first, Nationalist Party members tried to retain exclusive privileges. This led to walk-outs by opposition party members. The situation seemed to be headed to a constitutional crisis. But opposition members returned to the bargaining table and have achieved success in reversing unfair advantages enjoyed by the ruling party. They have relied on a growing democratic spirit in the country and have been able to persuade political rivals and the people of just principles that constitutional provisions must address. Peru's constitutional experience has not been as successful. President Fujimori selectively interpreted the constitution and strengthened his own power vis-à-vis the Congress and the courts. His actions undermined public confidence in the very idea of constitutional rule. It is now necessary in the wake of all the other challenges Peru faces, to reestablish constitutional norms.

Impact of the International Community

International actors can have a positive influence in offering incentives and rewards for consolidating democratic gains. The EEC rewarded membership to Southern European countries only after they were successful in consolidating their democratic regimes. NATO also encouraged allies to democratize to ensure that all members of the organization were defending common goals. Latin American countries had no equivalent to the EEC to offer them rewards for consolidating democracy, nor did they enjoy a military alliance to encourage reform within militaries as NATO did with Southern European countries. Only recently has the Organization of American States (OAS) shown interest in democratic development. High levels of debt and little incentive to curb borrowing has weighed heavily on infant democracies. Lending institutions have not always demonstrated a commitment to democratic development. At times they have supported austerity programs that have maintained or contributed to socioeconomic inequality. These are key reasons why Latin America has not had the same kind of success Southern Europe has had in consolidating democracy.[53]

In addition to international financial and security organizations, the foreign policies of neighboring democracies and of important countries like the United States can encourage consolidation. Established democracies can bring legitimacy to individual efforts to finish democratization by offering political and economic incentives. Both Taiwan and Peru have lacked access to powerful organizations like the IMF or military organizations like NATO that can encourage democracy. Still, both countries have been encouraged by the United States to develop their democratic institutions. Even though the United States and Taiwan have no official diplomatic ties, Washington's support for Taiwan's democracy was apparent in America's symbolic, yet dangerous, military move in the spring of 1996. Two American aircraft carriers took position off the Taiwan coast when Beijing attempted to intimidate Taiwan's leaders and voters with missile launches in the Taiwan Strait. The effort reaffirmed Washington's support for democracy in general and for the democratic aspirations of Taiwan's people. Peru has been a more difficult case for Washington. Despite the U.S. State Department's repeated criticisms of the Peruvian government for human rights violations, Washington recognizes that drug trafficking has been a problem in Peru, and they have supported Peru's use of the military to address the problem.

American leaders also believe that economic prospects for Peru initially improved under Fujimori and that Fujimori's authoritarian ways had considerable public support. On the other hand, Washington renewed its support for democracy in Peru by helping to finance the 2001 presidential elections and by offering increased aid to Peru for democratic advancements.[54] Pressure from international organizations and foreign governments will be more effective in Peru if the prospects for economic stability improve and if democratic reforms occur. Pressure will almost certainly continue, however, and the hope for a democratic Peru will continue.

These constitute major factors that most scholars find important in laying the groundwork for consolidating democracy. They are by no means exclusive. Many countries will struggle with these problems, or they will face unique problems that would not constitute worries in other countries. In spite of these useful characteristics of consolidation and the efforts of comparativists to capture the essence of democracy in the consolidation process, there is more that should be addressed in the consolidation process. We now turn to this discussion.

Critique and Conclusion

There is a marked difference in how comparativists write about transition and consolidation. It was argued in the preceding chapter that scholars too often tend to explain democratic transitions from the standpoint of democracy being the least objectionable or the only workable system of government after all other options have been exhausted. But in writing about consolidation, scholars like Linz and Stepan emphasize the difficulty of consolidating gains, which very often requires leaders to put aside personal policy preferences and people to support policies that may delay economic reforms that they sorely desire. Consolidation theorists also point to other qualitative aspects of democracy in terms of civic duties and attitudes that must prevail in order for democracy to thrive. In other words, the consolidation literature does a better job of arguing why people would favor democracy over authoritarianism than the transition literature does. Consolidation theory builds a case for democracy that is intellectually more satisfying than the transition literature. It helps us understand why authoritarians may come to agree that democracy is something that is superior to other regimes. The third wave of democracy is replete with examples of authoritarians who are finding it impossible to convince others that (the logic and promise of) democracy is inferior to "rule by the few." Many of these authoritarians have therefore stepped aside. Between 1995 and 1998, authoritarians in the Dominican Republic, El Salvador, Honduras, Nicaragua, Papua New Guinea, Romania, Mali, and Thailand agreed to greater political freedoms and allowed democracy to emerge.[55] The language that scholars have chosen to describe consolidation embodies the essence of democracy. They speak of issues of equality, justice, and improving people's lives. So while we have come to accept studying transition and consolidation separately for methodological reasons, we have also come to accept a different defense of democracy for the transition phase than we have of the consolidation phase. Democracy in the transition stage is simply initial democratic elections. Democracy in the consolidation phase is a whole range of qualities we deem important for living well in a democracy. Some might suggest that separating studies of transition and consolidation is warranted because there can be different kinds of elite behaviors and decisions made during democratic transitions than during periods of democratic consolidation. Still, scholars point out that serious obstacles to democracy that are not overcome in the period of democratic transition persist as attempts are made to consolidate democracy. Some of these problems can prevent consolidation from taking place, and authoritarianism may reappear. For democratizers the goal of democratic transition and consolidation is ultimately the same—to establish a strong, viable democratic regime. We also acknowledge that consolidation does not follow of a set pattern that occurs directly after a transition from authoritarianism. As pointed out in this chapter, Taiwan took significant steps toward democratic consolidation before the first fully free elections for president ever took place. Every case study suggests there are glaring exceptions, or at least qualifications that have to be made, in comparing general patterns of democratization to the experiences of individual countries. For this reason, the literature on consolidation teaches us something about transitions to democracy. We have come to accept transition and consolidation as two distinct processes, and as a result, we have competing justifications for explaining democratic development. How can we overcome this problem? It is not easy given that it does make sense to break democratization into two compartments, one leading to the first democratically held elections, and another that sees democratic attitudes and institutions take hold and begin to flourish. Perhaps the solution is in developing a consistent defense of democracy that abandons cynical and inaccurate perceptions about why transitions from authoritarianism to democracy occur. There is a better explanation of why transitions take place than trite claims that suggest "all other possibilities have been exhausted." There may be some truth in this, but there should also be some acknowledgement that faith in democracy prevails.

This brings us back to the concerns of the first chapter. Focusing on a definition of democracy that speaks to rights and virtues can help steer us clear of explanations that are inadequate. It helps us understand that transition and consolidation are attempts to describe an overall process that begins with the rejection of an inferior regime and the acceptance of a superior one. Our definition of democracy guides us to justifications for rights, attention to the theory of rights, and a fuller assessment of liberty in general. It causes us to consider more closely the virtues needed to support rights and to determine whether nor not a newly democratized regime will be able to develop a vibrant civil society where people live by democratic rules in their private associations and in their informal relations with others. The components of our definition of democracy move us beyond the exercise of identifying what factors make democracy the only game in town behaviorally, constitutionally, and attitudinally. They give us power to explain why people do or do not develop faith in democracy. In his analysis of the young American republic, Tocqueville considered elements that contributed to the consolidation of democracy in America. Scholars are beginning to appreciate just how significant Tocqueville's work is to understanding democratic consolidation and maintaining democracy.[56] They are right to look to civil society and the importance of institutions. But our literature on civil society and institutions tends to claim these ideas are important, but it does not tell us enough of the underlying factors that give rise to civil society. This requires us to pay more attention to how rights and virtues can be accepted or rejected in democratizing countries. This takes us back to a consideration of democratic philosophy.

I have already said that the literature on consolidation is better than the literature on transition precisely because it does contain a philosophy of democracy; but it can be improved. Understanding democratic consolidation means understanding how civil society develops. To understand how civil society develops, we must know how countries teach rights and virtues. The factors we mentioned that lead to consolidation are dependent upon enlightened leaders and citizens who grasp the ideal of democracy, not simply its barest trappings. This requires some appreciation of the concept of rights and the idea that courage, sacrifice, compassion, justice, equality, compromise, fair play, and wisdom are essential in consolidating a democracy. Rights and virtues lay the groundwork for justifying constitutional laws, encouraging leaders and citizens to behave as noble democrats should behave, and fostering attitudes about democracy that are vibrant and enduring. We come to appreciate why citizens can be trusted in a democracy. We see the difference good leadership makes. Our confidence in our own abilities to govern our personal lives and the nongovernmental organizations we belong to grows, and our quality of life improves. Democracy is accepted as being a noble and great way of governing, because it gets beyond concerns of raw political power. The dignity of individuals and our institutions is, after all, more than simply political power.

This kind of understanding can only be done by looking at democracy as a regime—as a way of living—and not simply as a way of being governed. Turning again to our definition as a measurement of democratic quality, we are led to ask certain fundamental questions about rights and virtues. How are rights taught? Are they accepted as legitimate by both leaders and citizens? What kinds of virtues are taught or are available within religious, family, and cultural traditions that can soften reliance on rights and encourage love for democracy and its institutions? How do democratic leaders define the good life and how does this relate to the ideal of democracy? How has the concept of the good life changed as democracy has evolved? These are important considerations. They justify changes and are catalysts that are essential to understanding every nation's acceptance of democratic principles.

If one takes a serious look at the philosophical justifications for democracy, we find the fundamental reasons why Prezworski's and other scholars' minimalist definitions of consolidation may not even address democratic concerns, but only trappings that are a part of what democracy as a concept embodies. Arguments about ethnocentrism fade as a consensus of democracy grows. We come to realize that the principles that we should esteem in North America and Western Europe are the kinds of ideas that all human beings can admire. We avoid setting low standards that insult the democratic consciences of courageous people striving for democratic excellence in all areas of the world. Democracy is a heritage born in the West, but one that can be common to all people.

The questions and concerns raised here are best handled in the next chapter. A fully consolidated regime is really an established democracy. In turn, the concerns of established democracies are really the same issues faced by countries in transit from authoritarianism to democracy and those struggling to consolidate democratic gains. Thus, we return to the fundamental concerns raised in the first chapter.

4

Maintaining Democracy

Like any other institution, a democratic republic needs maintenance. Most institutions like churches, governments, and private associations consider both the structural configuration of their organizations and the quality of their membership to be of paramount importance. For this reason, formal institutions usually draw up some sort of constitutional rules elaborating how they are to be structured and specifying the rights and duties of members. Usually there are also ideals that go beyond minimal requirements for membership. As stated in the first chapter, the ideals a democratic society thrives on include democratic virtues. To briefly review, virtues are those attributes that keep a citizenry from becoming too reliant on rights because rights will not always adequately curb selfish interests. The virtues important to a democracy include courage to uphold liberty, equality, and justice; loyalty to democratic principles; self-restraint to preserve the common good; generosity in thinking about others; a sense of individual and public justice; and prudence to know when and how to act. In large measure, virtues are based on an accepted standard of right and wrong that very often has its foundations in religious and ethical beliefs. In this chapter, I will show how the virtuous attributes a person develops on his or her own in the family and through religious teaching can contain elements essential for citizenship in a democracy. I will also show how distinct democratic virtues are taught in schools, through participation in private associations, and by democratic leaders.

This chapter is primarily concerned with the quality of the citizenry in republics. By quality, I mean the degree of virtue upheld by people living in democracies. Virtue in democracies has been and continues to be an essential concern of political philosophers. They are concerned with the conditions that are most conducive to the maintenance of virtue. Initially, this is directly related to the size of a republic.

Philosophers like Montesquieu believed that small republics were better than large republics because of his concern for maintaining virtue in republics. He believed the most apparent danger to a small republic was a large foreign force. He thought small republics could maintain peace because they could contain personal ambition and corruption better than a large republic could. Montesquieu believed that a small republic would be more likely to maintain public and private institutions that make democracy work. But a large republic, according to Montesquieu, is destroyed "by an internal vice."[1] He reasoned that a large republic would breed harmful factions that would result in unhealthy competitions for wealth and power, thus causing citizens to forget about the virtues needed to keep republics safe from destruction. He was not alone in his worries about size of democratic republics.[2] The American founders all took seriously the consideration of size of republics for fear of crafting a regime that might contain too many competing elements that could tear the republic apart.

The American founders took a bold step in showing that a large republic may, in fact, be more stable than a small republic. They believed large republics would invite more players, and thus more voices, into the political spectrum, which would lessen the chances of a dominant faction exceeding their democratic limits.[3] In essence, the founders were making the argument that the size of the republic was not a question of geography or population, but mainly one of maintaining democratic spirit. The political ideals of the people that made up the republic and the kinds of factions people formed were a reflection of what the citizenry deemed important. This would be true of large or small republics, though with a large republic it might be safer to assume that sound judgment would rule the day because reason would be more likely to steer the republic than if a single faction or a few dominant factions had their way. The emphasis on size and separation of government powers was important because of the desirability of preserving rights and because size was a concern in nurturing democratic virtues.

In reality, our consideration of democratic transitions and consolidation has done an adequate job of focusing on structural considerations. It is noted here only because of its relationship to democratic virtues, which, I will argue in this chapter, should be a pressing concern for comparativists as they study established democracies. In fact, I will make the argument that the difference between regimes in transitional and consolidating stages and regimes that are established democracies is the degree to which democratic virtues are nurtured. Established democracies move beyond immediate challenges to democracy. An established democracy is a democratic regime that is ever vigilant in keeping democratic hope alive. It instills in its citizens the dangers of becoming too complacent and accepting of rights in the absence of virtue. Established democracies teach about rights, but also about responsibilities, sacrifice, courage, and other virtues that are required of citizens and leaders alike to maintain democracy. While democratic transition and consolidation leads to a democratic ethic of respecting one another, established democracies develop deeper philosophical views of why democracy is the best regime. In established democracies, we should be looking to other sources for political leadership than we do in regimes experiencing transition or consolidating gains. Families, churches, schools, and private institutions ought to play key roles in maintaining democracy. It is a role that has been largely overlooked by comparativists. That is not to say that comparative political studies do not consider these institutions. Most comparativists have spent a tremendous amount of time looking at questions of political culture, the role of the family, religion, education, and so forth in democratic and nondemocratic regimes. I am suggesting that we need to spend more time looking at how all of these institutions teach virtues that nurture the regime rather than focusing on them as agents of socialization in general.

Trouble in the Established Democracies

At the very moment when the former communist-bloc countries are struggling to consolidate their democratic gains, the citizens of established democracies in North America, Western Europe, Japan, Australia, and New Zealand are expressing widespread disillusionment with their governments. A certain degree of cynicism has always been a part of democratic regimes. Politicians and policies are frequently a target of ridicule for political cartoonists, comedians, and everyday citizens. Still, leaders have been looked to for providing political leadership and even moral guidance on important issues of the day. But citizens of the world's established democracies are increasingly abandoning their respect for their democratic leaders and for the government institutions that serve the people. They complain that their leaders are corrupt, that they are out of touch with the person on the street. They complain that politicians dole out advantages to the rich, or to the poor, or to the middle class, without regard to the real needs of society as a whole. Citizens feel they lack power to reverse the direction of legislatures that cower to special interests.

Political scientists have written extensively about this phenomenon, but nobody is really sure of how dangerous it is to democracy in the near or distant future. They are not even sure of what *it* is. The theories political scientists use to explain the malaise are often no more sophisticated (nor need they be) than what is reported on the evening news. Some point to rising expectations of people living in democracies and the limits to economic growth and government's inability to improve the delivery of services. A few suggest that the problem is the loss of community and the sense of being alone in a world of super computers, super highways, and information overload. Others point to the media and its detrimental impact upon our basic values. A few complain that citizens living in established democracies have become spoiled—that they have too much and expect too much from governments that were designed to work at a deliberative pace and to provide limited services.[4] Some complain that a decline in "social capital," or trust and collective action, has weakened our democratic sensibilities.[5] Others suggest the decline of political parties has led to a disconnect between society at large and democratic institutions.[6]

Democratically elected leaders of these countries are very aware of the disengagement from politics their countrymen are experiencing. Anxious to satisfy unhappy constituents, politicians attempt to cut taxes without cutting popular social welfare programs. They pass laws that obligate bureaucracies to provide better environmental protection, inform citizens, improve educational test scores, provide childcare, and upgrade transportation systems. At the same time they work to enhance the environment for corporate research and development by providing tax breaks, market research, and subsidies for projects that will benefit governments and consumers. Even with all the tasks that leaders are called upon to perform, citizens very often fail to appreciate the hard work and commitment of their elected representatives. Instead, leaders are criticized for being corrupt, out of touch, and in government for their own selfish reasons. Whether it is Berlin, Washington, Ottawa, or Tokyo, few national leaders command the respect due the offices to which they have been elected. The British, the Japanese, the French, and the Australians all view their elected leaders as the problem. Indeed the "inside the beltway" characterization of American politics is easily transferable to most established democracies. While we citizens castigate our elected officials for being out of touch, we excuse ourselves from our own responsibilities for democratic governance and the democratic way of life.

The problems established democracies experience can be the same problems developing countries experience. In their struggle to establish the barest trappings of democracy, democratic leaders in developing countries fight to establish rights and a democratic compromise. A deep sense of democratic virtues has not yet been established in these countries, and democracy begins to work in many cases simply on the basis of satisfaction of the most basic political interests. In the world's established democracies, we have forgotten much of the emphasis on virtues and have become anxious to assert our rights—legal claims to satisfy our self-serving sense of justice. But the reliance on rights to hold democracy together is risky. It puts established democracies on the same footing as infant democracies—regimes struggling to maintain the most minimal of democratic requirements. The citizens and leaders of established democracies that rely on these minimal standards find it difficult to determine what is wrong with their regimes. Understanding in part that there are more than rights at stake, democrats turn to social problems in an effort to fix democratic regimes. And like the politician giving the stump speech on the campaign trail, we begin listing the problems we need to address in order to make our system work again.

- "We need to reduce crime by hiring more police, building more prisons, and making tougher laws so that our streets, schools, and public spaces are safe from criminals."
- "We must get our schools to work and train our children to compete in an ever complex world."
- "We need affordable health care and housing; then we can begin rebuilding our communities."
- "We need to provide incentives for families to stay together and disincentives for divorce and illegitimacy."

While there are legitimate concerns expressed in each item on this wish list, we bring the wrong tools in to fix these problems because the disease that is at the root of our democratic soul remains largely undiagnosed. What is the disease and why does it remain undiagnosed?

The fact is that established democracies do a pretty good job of addressing the very things we claim are the problems that we mention above. Recognizing the rise of violent and nonviolent crimes, democracies everywhere have passed laws and raised money to lower crime rates and have been successful in doing so (although few people living in democracies realize this). Democratic countries everywhere have been doing their best to increase educational test scores, especially in math and science, so that they can remain competitive and prosperous. Health-care schemes have been reformed and studied all over Europe and in the United States, and it continues to remain a priority of governments everywhere. Affordable housing is a major concern for governments as leaders struggle to find new ways to help people settle in communities. Family breakups have been a worry all over the industrialized world, especially in the established democratic states where single-parent families of divorce are changing our ideas of what constitutes a typical family. And while these problems have been studied in detail, and laws have been passed to stem the tide of political disaffection, other factors outside the direct realm of government legislation have done more to whittle away at our democratic foundations than our love-hate relationship with our democratically elected leaders.

The citizens of established democracies live in an age of disaffection because they are abandoning much of what holds a democratic regime together. At the outset of this book, it was claimed that democracy is a good regime because it makes people better. At the same time it was suggested that the responsibility to make people better was not merely a government responsibility. The argument here is not meant to support the claims of those who complain of government meddling in our lives. It is to suggest that so much of how we live our lives in a democratic regime is dependent on a complex interplay of factors that help us understand our duty to others. This obligation to others is not simply recognizing rights, it is shouldering responsibility that goes beyond rights. The maintenance of liberty is dependent on civil society, not simply government checks and balances. Civil society is in turn maintained by private institutions, associations, and our economic ties, and people's sense of proper behavior. Living in a civil society requires acts of generosity, occasional courage, and self-sacrifice. These virtuous acts are good not only in hopes that others will return such favors, but because they tame ambitions in ways that lend to the civility of life in democracies. It helps us realize that to be a truly free people, we must be free to perform acts that government does not require us to perform. To put it another way, a democratic regime is in a good state of repair if its citizens perform good deeds for society and are concerned for the welfare of society in ways that are not directly related to rights. Good deeds can be delivered in the form of direct service to the community or by helping at a school where one's children study, or to a community group that provides entertainment and amusement for the members of the group and the society at large. They are done by church groups, neighborhood groups, and by groups of individuals who join together to perform a single task. And they are performed by individuals who see a need and take it upon themselves to address this need.

Many would suggest this is an idyllic image that has existed in the imaginations of people but nevertheless one that has never existed and never will exist in reality. But those making such claims are the ones who are naïve and not those who call for a regime maintained by these virtues. Critics are right to raise such questions, however, because the greatest observer of the modern democratic regime worried about how long the world's first democracy could itself maintain its lofty democratic calling.

Tocqueville and the American Democratic Regime

In recent years there has been a rediscovery of Tocqueville's work on the American democratic regime.[7] This rekindled interest in Tocqueville is significant in that it indicates that political scientists are beginning to look once again at democracy as a regime in the grand sense—a political ideal that includes a government system, a civil life, and pays attention to the kinds of things people do as individuals and in families and groups that are not specifically political but nevertheless have political consequences. Tocqueville is arguably the most perceptive modern thinker who considers democracy. His study of the young American republic has given us a barometer to judge democratic regimes in general. While studies of democracy done by comparativists in the post–World War II period have rather limited use over time, Tocqueville's work, always popular with political philosophers, draws comparativists back to the main concerns of political science.

Tocqueville's intent was not identifying principles that were common to all regimes. He was fascinated with democracy and wanted to uncover the ideas and philosophy that empowered democracy. Already intimately familiar with the works of Hobbes, Locke, Montesquieu, and Hume, Tocqueville came to America to visit the laboratory of democracy. He wanted to see how its participants handled their liberties that guaranteed the right to pursue self-interest. He wanted to view up close the government institutions and determine how they related to the way normal Americans carried out their day-to-day lives. He was an outsider anxious to see how modern democracy compared to classical democracy and especially aristocracy. He hoped that his study could teach him something about his own country and the other countries of Europe. In a very real sense, *Democracy in America* is a work of comparative politics because the intention is to use the study of the American regime to study other regimes.

We are obliged to take Tocqueville's study seriously. Our comparative works have too often sacrificed the study of democratic virtues in our erstwhile attempts to understand government structures, interest groups, political parties, and political elites. Tocqueville not only studied all of these aspects of democracy, but he did so within the rubric of what he found most promising about democracy—that it was built upon a foundation of particular virtues that existed prior to the establishment of political institutions. These ideals gave rise to the idea of democracy, which is far more important to understanding the regime than focusing on the specific attributes of particular government organs, leaders, or specific policies.

America was fortunate to have a founding. What I mean by this is America had a philosophical and religious purpose for organizing a democratic regime. In this era of newly emerging democracies, most have an idea of what democracy is but do not articulate the ideal of democracy as clearly as it was articulated by the American founders. For this reason, the United States has always played a unique role among democracies and carries the honor and burden of being the world's greatest democracy, not simply because of its championing of democratic principles and virtues, but because these principles have been so carefully scrutinized by our founders and by Tocqueville. As comparativists have rediscovered Tocqueville, we have begun to see what a terrible oversight it has been to study other countries without consulting *Democracy in America*. It is essential, therefore, to consider Tocqueville's study on democracy in the United States in order to familiarize ourselves with those attributes that established democracies ought to exude.

Tocqueville saw an American republic that was flawed but promising. He was worried that Americans may be too taken with commercial enterprises, that they may turn too much to their own interests and not to the public good, and that Americans tended not to care too much for deeply intellectual pursuits. Still, he believed the American character was forgiving, open-minded, and could be nurtured. Hence, Americans were generally prosperous while maintaining moral lives. His work was not intended to simply be a description of conditions in America. Tocqueville succeeds in rendering a detailed study of the modern democratic republic that has use for studying democracy everywhere in the world. The regime he considered is really modern democracy and not simply democracy in the United States. For these reasons, it is essential to consider those things that Tocqueville finds most concerning and most promising about the modern democratic regime.[8]

While Tocqueville spent a good amount of time talking about the structure of the American government, his concern was not to rehash basic liberal principles and the genius of the separation of powers. What he was concerned about was maintenance of such a system of governance. Rather than focusing on the laws that are established to curb corruption and check power in the branches of government, Tocqueville was more concerned about other ways to limit the ambitions of men both in government and out of government. Indeed, this is the main concern of his work. This chapter will concentrate on Tocqueville's study of religion, the family, and political and civil associations and how these relate to freedom and equality. It will also consider Tocqueville's study of freedom and equality in conjunction with economics, the role of individuals in democratic societies, and how education must safeguard these principles in a democratic society.

Mores Animate Democracy

A central concern for Tocqueville was mores, sometimes referred to as habits of the heart. Mores, he argued, are human beings' opinions, ideas, and beliefs, "that shape mental habits." More than doing good deeds, mores are the moral and intellectual condition of a people.[9] Tocqueville believed that it was mores that govern democracy rather than simply laws. Mores and laws together create the opinions and customs necessary to support democracy. Dispositions that are not created by mores can at the very least be modified by mores. Human beings may not completely lose their petty ways or selfish interests, but mores help them find ways to limit the most harmful aspects of their proclivities.[10] They learn fairness, respect for others, and sportsmanship. Every child may want to win at a game, but through mores, children establish democratic rules that enable them to have an equal chance to win or lose with dignity. These good habits engendered by mores train children to work together to solve other problems, thus instilling a democratic means of problem solving that they use as adults.[11] Mores not only work to the self-interest of those living in a democracy, they also establish a citizenry that is patriotic—proud of their rights and their ethical ways of treating one another. Without mores, rights would be self-destructive, and citizens in a democracy would view the state in ever less-respectful ways. Esteem for one another would decline, and selfish interests would rule over reason. Ultimately Tocqueville believed such a condition could lead to the ruination of democracy.[12]

But this is not to imply that Tocqueville believed that democracy would provide the best for human beings under all circumstances. He believed that democracies have limited abilities to change human beings in certain key areas. He thought the nature of democracy made it impossible to cure men of their material desires. He complained that democrats were not likely to be intellectual leaders nor producers of fine art. But he did believe that, in general, democracy could bring about a genteel nature in human beings that could not be matched in countries where aristocratic regimes allowed only a few to enjoy the good things in life while depriving the majority of a good way of life.

> [I]f in your view the main object of government is not to achieve the greatest strength or glory for the nation as a whole but to provide for every individual therein the utmost well-being, protecting him as far as possible from all afflictions, then it is good to make conditions equal and establish a democratic government.[13]

Religion and Its Connection to Democratic Mores

Establishing democratic government means establishing rights and a republican form of government. Even more important, however, it means finding a way to make the most of and foster democratic mores. These mores, according to Tocqueville, had a direct connection to religion, particularly Christianity. He believed that Christianity varied in its contribution to democracy, depending on the denomination. Christianity did not control the government by merging government with a particular religion. Instead, Tocqueville believed the fervency of religious faith of America's founders made Christianity "the first of their political institutions."[14]

Religion is important for several reasons. Tocqueville believed Christianity had a practical side, a moral side, and a philosophical side that suited democracy's interests well. On the practical side, he believed that Christianity's teachings asserting that all people are equal before God, provided the justification needed to establish the idea that all citizens, regardless of their circumstances, were equal before the law.[15] Americans either believed in Christianity or felt obliged to appear to be believers, thus establishing a common moral thread that could bind people together prior to the establishment of democratic institutions. Those who did not believe in Christian tenets could see that it was good and would therefore not feel inclined to challenge the beliefs of others. At the same time, those who did believe were likely to be vocal defenders of their beliefs, thus promoting Christian tenets throughout society.[16]

Christianity benefits from the political give-and-take of democracy as well. While Tocqueville acknowledged that in the moral world of Christianity everything was "decided in advance" according to commandment and the will of God, politics was unpredictable, contested, and was best when discussed passionately from a variety of perspectives.[17] This opposition creates a harmony that is well suited to human beings using their reason, backed by a moral inclination to do good in the pursuit of public policy. So while political decisions naturally give rise to debate, religion rules hearts in a way that allows for compromise. Religion is the "guardian of mores," which maintains freedom and equality.[18] Laws and secure borders are simply not enough. Good mores, instilled by religious and moral teachings, remind citizens of what is reasonable. The laws may allow questionable behavior, but religion "forbids them to dare."[19] Religion, therefore, does not make the laws, but it directs behavior through the teaching of mores. Christianity provides the first and best protections of equality and freedom and is not merely a supplement to law.

Tocqueville's belief that religion nurtures and protects freedom and equality contradicted the usual view of religion held by many at the time of his visit to America. It is also a point of contention today. Many scholars consider religion to be a pernicious influence on democracy and free inquiry. But Tocqueville argued that religious freedom would help maintain liberty. If men are free to worship as they please, they would grant these and other liberties to their fellow citizens. This is claimed to be true for both Protestantism and Catholicism. Tocqueville found that by declaring religious liberty in America, both Protestants and Catholics were loyal democrats. Being loyal to principles of equality, American

Catholics had a natural love for democratic institutions because all citizens were equal before God. Such observances led Tocqueville to declare that all Christian religions, provided they were true (i.e., sound in conventional doctrine and teaching men to lead virtuous, tranquil lives), would have power over men's souls and make them friendly to democracy.[20] Without religion, Tocqueville was concerned that uncertainty, instability, and confusion would be so great that America's freedom and sense of equality would be jeopardized. Despotism could do without religious faith, but the institutions of freedom depended on religion to keep humans from taking excessive advantage of their freedom for selfish purposes. For this reason, Tocqueville believed that religion was not simply desirable, but necessary for the maintenance of democracy.[21]

Going hand-in-hand with the practical is Christianity's philosophical support for democracy. Tocqueville is not the only philosopher who acknowledges the role Christianity played in the Enlightenment. He is more assertive than others, however, in suggesting that Christianity contains divine laws that establish liberty among human beings. He makes this assertion in his observations of American Puritans. Upon landing in America, the Puritans immediately organized, using their religious beliefs as a political theory. They built their governing bodies on the basis "of an idea" where they could seek God in freedom. Thus they established laws and customs "as if they were dependent on God alone."[22] This naturally led to a situation where Americans participated in politics willingly, made their own decisions regarding taxes, established trial by jury, and required personal responsibility of themselves. Thus the new American republic grew locally first and then led to the establishment of larger political units later (the reverse of what often happens when a country develops democratically today).[23] Tocqueville's assertion that Christianity creates a philosophical justification is not deeply philosophical in the sense that a central philosophical concept is discovered or developed by democratic people but, rather, that democracy emerges because of the intellectual justifications that grow out of Christianity. Hence the relative ease with which early American settlers established institutions that were both morally grounded in Christian principles and democratic in spirit.

Doctrinally, Christianity provides a larger view of the purposes of life that prevents people from demanding too much from their government and their liberal rights. Tocqueville found that Americans believed more in the afterlife than did Europeans. People everywhere commonly held views about eternity and God's purposes. This helped people to put aside their petty desires and to focus on goals that were unobtainable in this life—beyond the abilities of democracy to deliver.[24] With fixed ideas about God, their righteous standing, and their duties toward God and others, Americans were more likely to bridle passions that would harm democracy. Tocqueville believed that these set ideas about good and evil were more important than any other beliefs the people held.[25] It was good for individuals, not simply for the preservation of the regime.

The Christian doctrine of all being equal in God's eyes is especially useful for maintaining the idea of equality. Tocqueville believed Americans demonstrated the ideal that equality is a passion that is eternal. Being equal to one other, therefore, gives Americans a satisfaction every day that they are both Christian and democratic. But Tocqueville was also deeply worried about the evils of equality. He believed extreme equality could be a serious problem because it would produce mediocrity and apathy. To check these evils, Tocqueville believed liberty was essential to counter both the threat to rights that comes from an equal society that might otherwise produce conditions of mediocrity and apathy.[26]

As is evident from the foregoing discussion, Christianity is not only important to democracy because of its practical applications; it was for Tocqueville at the heart of a healthy democratic regime. But the problem remains: How is religion taught by political leaders, and how is Christianity to be taken seriously in countries where its hold is not strong? Tocqueville agreed with the American founders that faith must be a personal choice, and no state religion should be established. In fact, Tocqueville believed that people were more likely to love religion if they were free to believe rather than following a religion that was an arm of state power.[27] He argued it was the duty of every lawgiver to get men to look to God and take religion seriously. Still, he acknowledged that it was difficult at best for political leaders to get people to take spiritual matters seriously.[28] He did believe that democratic beliefs impart religion by making religious truths (like personal responsibility, rewards for hard work, equality) identifiable in this life and not simply in the afterlife.[29] And he believed political leaders must act as if they believe in immortality and practice religion in order to teach its precepts to others. But in the long run, Tocqueville believed that when it came to determining how they should live their lives, the people in a democracy should already have fervent Christian beliefs that provide external guidance beyond the laws of democracy.

Democracy's Nursery: The Family

From the foregoing discussion, it is plain to see that religion plays a dominant role in the American democracy Tocqueville observed in the early nineteenth century—not by intervening in the state, but by establishing a democratic ethic. Close to religion in importance was the family. The family is a nursery of democratic citizenship. The family plays a different role in a democratic regime than in an authoritarian regime. As Tocqueville pointed out, families in monarchies learn to defer to parental authority and not to question the wisdom of commands given by fathers, just as subjects do not question the commands of the monarch. But just as the connection of the traditional family in Europe can be made to monarchy, the family in America teaches principles that make us better citizens in democracy. The roles of men and women in the United States differed from those of their counterparts in Europe. Tocqueville believed that while fathers ultimately made decisions on weighty matters in American families, they were more likely to listen to the counsel of their wives and children than fathers in Europe. He credits women for the central role of teaching mores in the home. Women's fervent belief in religion and their concern for the children's well-being have a profound impact on marriage and the family. They are the key agents for shaping mores in the home, though their desires are reinforced by their husbands, who demonstrate religious faith by practicing these mores in and out of the home.

Though families in both the United States and Europe were mostly engaged in farming, Tocqueville noted that Americans did not have a peasant mentality, and in fact, could not fathom what peasant life was like. He notes that this was not because of schools or the government, but because parents taught their children by word and deed how to be a democrat by relying on their religion, freedom, and equality.[30] While the European household taught the necessities of rank and privilege, the American household had a democratic quality where parents and children enjoyed each other's company and participated to a significant degree in making decisions as a family. Tocqueville noted the ease with which Americans regarded home as a refuge from the world. After the day's duties are over, the head of the house returns home, and there "all his pleasures are simple and natural and his joys innocent and quiet, and as the regularity of life brings him happiness, he easily forms the habit of regulating his opinions as well as his tastes."[31] Again, much of the

119

sanctity of the home is because of religious belief. Tocqueville suggested that Americans practiced their religion in their homes by keeping their "hearth and bed sacred" and by building lives for families that were a "perfect picture of order and peace."[32] Though Tocqueville's description seems rosy-eyed even for nineteenth-century America, his point is important. The family in America was far more likely to educate children on matters practical and moral than families in Europe because its understanding of equality and freedom suggests responsibility for doing so. The family is therefore a nursery for teaching moral and ethical virtues that have application in public life.

Into the Public Realm—Political and Civil Associations

In addition to learning democracy through family contact, Tocqueville emphasized the importance of associations and their relation to American democracy. Like religion, Tocqueville boldly asserted that nations that are democratic have no chance of surviving without associations. Associations engage the public, inform the citizenry, and prevent the creation of secret societies that imperil freedoms.[33] For these reasons, Tocqueville was encouraged to find that Americans formed institutions of all kinds and all sizes. Although most were not organized with a political purpose, he noted the importance of every institution to the maintenance of democracy. Religions, commercial associations, garden clubs, and so on, all provided interests that brought people together. Once these associations were organized, members governed themselves by democratic rules—electing leaders, reaching compromise decisions, and regulating their own affairs. Thus, like the family, associations perform the function of teaching and emphasizing democratic rules of behavior for deciding a course of action to take and settling issues of conflict. But Tocqueville noted another important role that associations played. A society that is blessed with many free associations was not likely to be bothered by the dangerous pursuits of powerful persons. In Europe he noted captains of commerce and political leaders were likely to intervene often in the affairs of people, but where associations exist, a new culture emerges that creates an artistry of people working together to address interests and concerns.[34] These associations countered the tendency toward individualism. Private associations also helped preserve the ideal of limited government. If private associations could adequately address some of the most pressing needs of society, the government was less likely to intervene, thus preserving the invigorating role of citizens in a democratic republic. A limited government was therefore less likely to infringe upon the liberties of the people.[35]

Some political associations were necessary to ensure the independence and freedom of civil associations. Political associations include all those associations whose direct purposes are political. They include political parties, intellectual societies that pursue political purposes, and all other associations organized for political purposes. While Tocqueville held deep reservations over associations such as political parties, he nevertheless deemed them essential for maintaining political freedoms.[36] Without them, independent political views are not likely to be articulated. Policies would be established by governments without public discussion and without their harmful influences discussed prior to their implementation. Political ambitions would not be checked by the suspicions of others, and government would be more likely to operate behind a veil of secrecy. So political associations, representing the interests and concerns of citizens from all walks of life, would stand as a guardian of rights and the public interest. If they are not allowed to exist, no institution, not even civil associations of a nonpolitical nature, are safe from interference.

Equality and Freedom in the Economy and Special Challenges to the Individual

Tocqueville reinforces the feelings of the American founders in arguing that free economic institutions can be a training ground for democracy and an outlet to channel people's ambitions. A free economic system satisfies people's desires for independence and their desire to live prosperous lives. Allowing people to own property helps to reinforce bourgeois ideals. And people engaged in economic pursuits can easily see how self-interest overlaps with the public interest. In order to prosper, one must participate in the economic life of the community where one is rewarded by playing by the rules that govern economic life. This also has a complementary effect on combating isolation which can, in Tocqueville's mind, destroy a democracy.[37] But a free economic system can also strip men of rank and privilege that is enjoyed by the few in an authoritarian regime. It leaves people with only wealth by which to distinguish themselves, which can be offset by Christian principles. Tocqueville believed that Americans sought material wealth to a great degree but were kept from ruining themselves by their love for "moral delights."[38] In this regard self-interest is safeguarded by the principle of equality. People may want property, power, and wealth, but the principle of equality limits their ambitions by reminding people to consider what is essential instead of what is possible. It also whets the appetites of the ambitious by rewarding them with immediate wealth, thus removing some of the curiosity of wealth.[39] With more people going after wealth, limits are further placed on what people can expect to learn, thus teaching them to expect a modest rather than a great fortune.

But the quest for wealth still bothered Tocqueville deeply. The drive for wealth and material comforts can be more than just a nuisance for democracy, it can be a destructive influence. Democracy is in better hands if its leaders are gentle and virtuous. They should respect mores and believe in them intensely. Tocqueville believes they should oppose materialism in all of its forms, be it economic or scientific.[40] Materialism causes men to put principles like equality aside. It causes them to overlook moral and religious teachings and therefore take mores lightly. Rather than seeking home as a refuge and engaging in public life with a range of interests, excess materialism makes people methodical in their single-minded approach to wealth and all its trappings. It creates a society without variety, without character, and causes people to withdraw from the public domains of democracy.[41] At best, an individual in such a situation strikes out on his own and reaps the benefits of his own labor but begins to retreat from all of the other aspects that democracy affords. In time, the mores that have taught gentleness and tranquility begin to ebb.

Individual rights in a modern democracy are to be revered. But rights by themselves are not enough. Tocqueville suggests that the principles of equality must be upheld so that individuals learn to think of others in ways other than by contractual rights. Tocqueville observed that the equality of the American republic brought a gentleness to rank-and-file Americans. As equal citizens, Americans more easily identified with their neighbors' happiness, misery, and common needs. This gave rise to a sense of compassion that helped people transcend some personal desires in order to lend a hand to those in need. At the same time, it buoyed up the confidence of democrats as they felt free to express opinions to one another. Yet amid this frankness, each person recognized the need to allow others to speak more out of courtesy than simply the right of free speech.[42] Thus a combined advantage for all in treating each other with civility and tolerance, coupled with the basic framework of rights in an equal society, comprised the principle Tocqueville described as "self-interest rightly understood." To be a virtuous person an individual must sacrifice something for another person. This not only satisfied Christian sensibilities, but serviced rights as well.[43] Tocqueville did not quibble about whether or not such behavior was altruistic or truly compassionate. Instead he argued that it led to a path that would ensure true happiness. While a fair degree of self-interest was involved in people's behavior, enlightened self-love was the essence of self-interest rightly understood.[44]

It would be incorrect, however, to think that doing good deeds for others was somehow just a superficial way of serving one's own desires. Tocqueville suggested self-interest rightly understood was based on an ideal that is larger than individual needs. The religious underpinnings of society and the mores that the people respected formed a foundation for people to concentrate on the day-to-day needs of their lives within the context of larger purposes. The eternal worries of Americans keep them from the worst behavior that would otherwise be possible in a liberal society. And Christianity teaches that people should put the needs of others first. Because people believed in Christian principles, they relied on these principles to order their lives as much as, if not more than, civil law. A citizen in the American republic assumed his neighbor was Christian and therefore believed that he feared God as much as he did. Certain acts of charity and concern for others were done for the love of God, which helped the individual free himself of petty pleasures. Sabbath observance meant people retired to their homes to read the Bible and did not open businesses.[45] For all of these reasons, self-interest rightly understood would not necessarily lead to exceptionally great deeds performed regularly on behalf of others. But perhaps, more importantly, it provided civility by teaching people to be moderate, temperate, and self-controlled in their daily comings and goings, which is essential to the vitality of democracy.[46] So selfishness and greed could be found in America but not in its ugliest forms because egoism was enlightened by self-interest rightly understood.

But Tocqueville worried about whether Americans could keep self-interests within bounds. Could the young republic keep people focused on the mores necessary to keep self-interest rightly understood? The greatest threat to self-interest being rightly understood was extreme equality. As affluence and the workaday atmosphere of the American republic persisted, Tocqueville correctly saw that Americans might become comfortable in their lives and feel that they owe nothing to others and expect nothing in return. They would come to discount the importance of democratic mores in society. The relative ease of making a good living in America could lead to others turning away from society and exclusively seeking the refuge of family and a few friends, thus losing their attachment to society. The short-term effects would not seem too detrimental to the republic. At first the individual who withdraws from society seeks refuge by being with friends and family. But as he retreats into this isolation, he forgets the reasons why contact with associations and the mores that drive men toward community are important. He increasingly seeks isolation from his peers. In time, Tocqueville worried that this would lead to egoism, a condition worse than individualism because the person who has withdrawn from society puts himself above others.[47] The attachment to mores is lost and petty disputes become serious chasms that pull at the fabric of democracy. Egoism and a loss of those mores that are supported by religion lead to hedonism. The individual, guided only by selfish desires, has forgotten about and no longer fears eternal condemnation. Turning completely to his own desires, he acts as if each day were his last. The virtues of moderation, tolerance, and self-interest rightly understood are seen as bothersome limits to his liberal rights. He comes to rely almost exclusively on his legal protections while abandoning the principles that make a democratic regime work at the civic level. Widespread disaffection from public life is not an attribute of democracy, but one of authoritarianism. Keeping men from joining together for mutual aid and benefit, the despotic ruler is able to call the political shots. For this reason, Tocqueville worried that democracy, left only to the contractual arrangements based on rights, seriously endangered liberty and left the regime ripe for decline.[48]

Citizens and Democratic Education

In order to prevent the collapse of democratic regimes, citizens and leaders must be fully educated in the virtues necessary to sustain democracy. This is done at many levels: the family, by government leaders themselves through thoughtful governance and example, by participation in political and civic associations, by religious teachings, and in the schools. Educating citizens in the economic and political opportunities their regime affords them is important. But there also needs to be a deliberate effort to instill in citizens a faith that the truth prevails in democracy. This is not to suggest that democracies will be immune from making poor decisions. But citizens need to be assured that even policies they may disagree with will prove to be wrong and therefore invite correction, or prove to be somewhat wrong but not threatening to the regime, or prove to be correct.[49] A large share of the duty for teaching this faith in democracy rests with enlightened leaders. Tocqueville believed the first duty of elected leaders was not simply to legislate but to educate citizens in a democracy. In particular, he thought leaders needed to do what they could to "purify mores." Tocqueville was well aware of the dangers of democracy. He believed that in spite of the fine attributes he had found in the American republic, democracy had nevertheless been "left to its wild instincts" and had grown up "like those children deprived of parental care who school themselves in town streets and know nothing of society but its vices and wretchedness."[50] The family, so influential in perpetuating opinions of political regimes, could be a force for good or evil in a democratic regime. Associations tend to teach the biases of the members who found them or the members who set agendas. For this reason, political leaders have a special need to shape mores and public opinion so that the civic life of the regime remains gentle, forgiving, and public spirited. This is not an easy task knowing that majority opinion can be cynical and at times critical of democratic mores. But Tocqueville believed the American republic demonstrated that the majority of Americans, though lacking polish and sophistication, was nevertheless politically savvy and more enlightened than the majorities living in the countries of Europe.[51]

In addition to enlightened political leaders and schools that teach civic responsibility, Tocqueville believed religion played a vital role in educating citizens. In his travels throughout the United States, he found the people of New England to be better citizens than other Americans because they were better educated. This was not because they spent more time in the schoolhouse. Rather, Tocqueville believed New Englanders were more enlightened because they had been better informed through religious teachings than Americans living elsewhere. Their teachings also emphasized principles of living in a free society. Being grounded in religious tenets and the liberal arts, Tocqueville believed liberty was better protected in New England because citizens better understood their responsibilities to one another as Christians first and then as citizens.[52]

CHAPTER 4

Are Tocqueville's Concerns Appropriate for
Contemporary Studies on Democracy?

Tocqueville believed that a new political science was necessary to take account of democratic change—a new political science that would help us find reasons why material progress could be made in some countries even though democracy fails to emerge. He felt we needed to uncover ways to calm new republics where democratic revolution causes men to waiver in their commitment to democracy. In comparing democracy to the crumbling monarchies of Europe, Tocqueville lamented that the intellectuals and political leaders of his day were out of touch with the realities of the world around them. "Carried away by a rapid current, we obstinately keep our eyes fixed on the ruins still in sight on the bank, while the stream whirls us backward—facing toward the abyss."[53] In some respects the same can be said of comparativists today. We have relied too much on our recent scholarship. Though we are not fixed on monarchy, we remain fixed on the social science methods of recent decades that keep pointing to the same kinds of phenomena. We are adept at measuring attitudes, trends, legislative issues, and problems of government structure, but not so adept at understanding democracy as an interplay of rights and virtues. For this reason, we continue to identify and treat the symptoms with which established democracies wrestle rather than studying and defending the basic components Tocqueville identified—the very components that constitute democratic regimes.

It is true, however, that critics might disagree with this assessment. After all, haven't scholars been concerned about the same things Tocqueville was concerned about? Mores are taken seriously nowadays. As mentioned earlier, there is a large and ever growing body of literature on social capital and the attributes societies need to make democracy work. For the most part, religion is viewed favorably again as a contributor to social capital instead of a threat to democratic freedoms. Scholars and policymakers alike have taken seriously the breakup of traditional families and the decline of quality in family life in general. The new institutionalism of political science is not so new anymore. It has been a focus of serious study for several decades. Issues of equality have always been important, especially regarding income distribution and social welfare principles. Many social scientists have expressed concern over the growing separation of individuals from public life. Education has been hotly debated as communities wrestle to educate citizens so that they will be economically productive and publicly engaging. Indeed, it could be argued that political scientists have done a remarkable job of addressing the very concerns Tocqueville addresses in his study of the young American republic. So what is the concern?

The problem is that while real progress has been made, comparativists are fixed on addressing different aspects of these issues than Tocqueville does. A popular conclusion comparativists forward in explaining the loss of public spiritedness in established democracies is to point to general dissatisfaction with policy performance in relation to popular expectations. Citizens show support for democracy in general but do not approve of the way government does its work.[54] Attempts are made to show how popular expectations have developed the way they have and why governments find it so difficult to meet such high and varied demands. But such conclusions do not get to the root problems of democratic governance the way Tocqueville's study does. Robert Putnam has taken an approach that does emphasize some of the very things with which Tocqueville is concerned. In fact, his work on Italy is in many ways reminiscent of Tocqueville's study of America in that he attempts to identify the character of civic life in modern Italy.[55] He traces key religious, cultural, political, and economic influences that have shaped the quality of Italian democracy. In general, Putnam suggests economic demands, mobility, family decay, and technological change have had a profound impact on modern democracies. His prescription is to look more closely at the kinds of associations that promote "horizontal ties" because of the promising impact this has on civic life in general. He is concerned with the way associational involvement has changed. And he wants us to consider how traditional sources of social capital have been impacted by our economic and government policies.[56] But Putnam's work has been criticized because it tends to look at components of civil society as being separate from political institutions. Critics point out that a democratic society is comprised of political institutions and civil associations, political and nonpolitical, that interact in a complex fashion.[57] Civil society does not necessarily lead to democratic behavior. In some cases political institutions limit the potential for "bad social capital," that is, collective behavior that is civilly based, but not conducive to democracy. Without this interplay of liberal political institutions and civil association, even bird-watching clubs and choral societies can become a tool of anti-democratic objectives.[58] Noticeably absent in all these studies, however, is a discussion of mores in general. Tocqueville agrees with Putnam that associations are vital for sustaining democracy. And he agrees with other studies that rising expectations create problems in democracy when the government is unable to meet popular demands. But for all of these concerns, Tocqueville encourages us to study mores and their impact on the key principles of equality and freedom. It is this kind of direct approach to mores—the virtues of democracy—that is missing in these studies. Our current methods remain useful, but not as profound or as fully informed about the threats to democracy as they should be.

In researching this book, nothing has struck me with greater force than the kind of attention Tocqueville places on religion and its connection to democracy. This is a difficult area for comparativists. We have avoided religion and its relationship to democracy because comparativists have at best held ambivalent feelings about religion and its connection to democracy. Christianity teaches respect for authority and can be used to crush the rights of those who have differing beliefs, whether they be religious or not. Some suggest it is not Protestantism, but Catholicism, Islam, and other orthodox religions that are unfriendly to democracy. Are these assumptions correct? Is religion as detrimental to democracy as comparativists often believe it to be? Is it all religion that is viewed in this way or every religion except Christianity?

We could consider Tocqueville's study of Christianity in the young American republic as valuable for determining what factors helped establish democracy at that time but realize its lack of importance to democracy now. In other words, we cannot get people to interpret religions in ways that are alien to them, but we recognize the relationship Tocqueville identified between religion and self-interest rightly understood. So maybe we can find alternative ways to develop self-interest rightly, so democracy not only persists but thrives. We could challenge scholars to look at how policies, economic dislocation, and technology have impacted Americans' desires to associate in civic institutions. This, of course, assumes that America and other established democracies are not likely to rekindle the religious fervor that Christianity enjoyed in early nineteenth-century America, and we must therefore substitute it for something else. Humanist principles could replace religion and perhaps do a better job of teaching people to look out for the good in each other because they would not carry the prejudice of religious difference.

But such claims are difficult to support in our world. We have been able to document decline in the quality of our public life and the higher demands citizens are making on their governments. We have looked just about everywhere but to religion to consider the health of democratic regimes. There are a few exceptions. Putnam calls for clergy, lay leaders, and worshippers to create a new "great awakening" so that social capital will be created.[59] Huntington has for some time pointed to the positive influence of Christianity and the prospects for democratization.[60] But he has held reservations about Catholicism and Islam. Recent studies agree with Tocqueville's work that Catholicism can be a help to democracy.[61] Other scholars are suggesting that Islam is compatible with democracy.[62] These studies are based on doctrinal issues and their relation to practical politics and provide useful insights into religion and its support for democracy. But they do not look at issues of faith and democracy with the same care and detail that Tocqueville does. Tocqueville identifies reasons why he thinks Christianity is essential to the maintenance of democracy. Contemporary scholars look at these religions in a general fashion without connecting them in detail to the mores of society and democracy. And they focus more on the development of democratic institutions and not necessarily long-term quality-of-life issues related to democracy. In this regard, we have much work to do. We need to better determine what, specifically, it is about Christianity that made it compatible with democracy when Tocqueville studied it and in what ways these principles still hold true today. Doing so will help us assess more accurately the mores that uphold civic life and give deep meaning to life in a democratic regime. We also need to determine if religions other than Christianity have the ability to move people toward democracy and sustain it. Our studies of Islam are not yet conclusive on this point.

My point here is not to suggest that religion should be our only focus for studying democracy. To make such a claim would be short-sighted and simply wrong. But while I believe we are making progress in studying institutions, family life, the role of individuals, and education in democracies, we have been reluctant to do serious studies of religion in established democracies. This oversight has prevented us from more fully understanding the problems with which institutions, families, and individuals struggle in complex modern societies. Just because our problems have become more complex does not mean that we should avoid fundamental questions about religion and God. Without a serious consideration of religion, we are at best looking at only part of the picture. But our studies remain woefully inadequate compared to the depth of insight and understanding about modern democracy that Tocqueville gave us. To do better we must change the way we study democracy in established and developing democracies. We need to do so by trying to answer Tocqueville's call for a new political science and consider how we look at and teach democracy.

Focusing on Virtues to Understand Modern Democracy

All democracies need continuous nurturing to develop and stay vibrant. The principles that move democracies from transition to consolidation are the same principles that move democracies from consolidation to maturity and maintain that maturity. We have too often looked at problems that challenge weak democracies to be different problems than the ones faced by mature democracies. Drawing from our discussion of Tocqueville in the previous section, it is important to look at how democracies are nurtured. In particular, what is it that we should look for as we go about studying established and new democracies? Not surprising, we need to focus on how democratic mores are taught, for it is mores that lend support to or challenge the assumptions that are made about a democratic regime.

In *Politics*, Aristotle suggests that a good citizen of a democratic regime needs to know both how to rule over others and how to be ruled.[63] In order to do this a citizen must know what virtues are important for the maintenance of the regime. Good democracies teach many things. They teach that citizens need to have a sense of fair play; that justice should be pursued both in public life and in private affairs; that people should love the truth and feel an obligation to search for the truth. Just as people seek justice and equality in a regime, they can also seek to establish regimes that honor hierarchy and authority. For this reason democracy should teach individuals who live in democracy to look out for the needs of others. Democracies should teach selflessness and a sense of sacrifice for the good of others. A democracy should teach citizens that they must be ruled but also be free. It should teach people how to be masters over their own lives and to be responsible to others.

As Tocqueville suggested, teaching these qualities requires a multifaceted approach. As comparativists, we need to assess how well the countries we study are doing in teaching these ideals. Religions and families teach individual virtues. These virtues may be inherently democratic but are primarily concerned with making people moral individuals. We first focus on this attribute—the development of virtuous individuals—then turn to the development of democratic virtues and citizenship. These include a discussion of the role of schools, associations, and leaders in teaching democratic virtues. There is a link between individual virtue and democratic virtues, but because the purposes of each may not be the same, they are treated separately in this discussion. Looking at these factors in this way, we will not only be better able to determine the level of support for democratic institutions of governance, but gain better insight into the overall quality of the regime in regards to the standards Tocqueville identified in his study of the young American republic. I will not repeat the reasons why each area is important but, rather, offer some open-ended suggestions to studying democratic regimes.

Individual Virtues and Religion

In the preceding section it was suggested that there is a direct link between Christianity and principles of equality and freedom. Much of this has to do with practical, philosophical, and doctrinal aspects of Christianity that lend support to the assumptions that human beings are equal in the eyes of God and therefore see equality as an eternal concept. At the same time, Christianity has the obligation to teach people to do the right thing without compulsion. This means that freedom is not license but, rather, an opportunity to choose wisely the way to live one's life. In studying democratic regimes we need to identify religious principles that do these things. How seriously do people take religion? Are the most prominent religious principles that people believe in conducive to democratic governance, or do they teach reliance on external authority to determine their moral standing in society? Do they teach equality of all, or do they seek to maintain rank and privilege in society? Are the religious principles taught by churches widely accepted or are people suspicious, disinterested, or selective in their adherence to doctrinal beliefs? Is the variability of belief likely to lend support to or detract from democratic mores?

Individual Virtues and Family Life

Comparativists have been too willing to accept the work of sociologists and anthropologists in studying families. While this has merit if one is studying nonpolitical aspects of family life, the family has been and always will be the nursery of political regimes. It is no surprise that in authoritarian countries, parents, and in particular fathers, have a stronger hold over their families than do parents in democratic societies. While the relative liberty of family life in democracies causes alarm among some authoritarian rulers, family life, as demonstrated by Tocqueville, can be extremely genteel in a democratic society. In the family the principles that parents find most important are taught to children. If religious and moral principles in general support or detract from democratic mores, comparativists need to be aware of these conditions. It is in the family that we most readily learn how important certain mores are and what benefits or challenges they will create for a democratic society.

In studying family life we need to determine what the foremost principles of the ideal family are in the country we study. Is the home a place where people want to be to seek happiness and contentment? Or is home life stressful because of extreme poverty and fear of local and national authorities? Do family members have a sense of belonging, or do they primarily recognize obligations and duties? Are public kindnesses and responsibilities taught in the home? Do parents see each other as partners and children as contributing members of the family unit? Are religious principles taught both out of eternal concern and to promote self-interests rightly? Is the divorce rate high and family life stressed because of the competing interests of individuals in the family? If so, how are mores taught?

Democratic Virtues and Schools

Schools are able to take the principles that children are taught in churches, the home, and society and put them directly to use in the form of civic education. It is important to identify how education leaders go about teaching democracy. Some established democracies have decided to focus more on vocational pursuits at the expense of liberal arts because they are deemed to contain more economic promise. Newer democracies often teach the same political history they taught prior to the transition to democracy, thus losing an ideal opportunity to plant the seeds of democracy. With these considerations in mind, various questions arise. What are the principles schools deem most important in regards to educating their citizens? Do they emphasize math and science to build the economy, or is there a real attempt to teach democracy as the best regime? If so, how is this taught? What heroes are identified, what are their contributions reported to be, what principles do they teach, and how effective is democratic education?

Democratic Virtues and Associations

Scholars like Putnam have done a good job of demonstrating why associations, public and private, are important to democracy. We need to study these associations from the standpoint of their being institutions that regulate society outside the bounds of government. They keep us free by allowing us to pursue our concerns and interests in freedom. We need to determine if the countries we study believe in associations. Are there all kinds of associations, both private and public, organized for a variety of purposes? Are people free to meet and run their affairs without fear of interference from other associations or the government? Do people rely on associations to do work instead of the government doing work? Do people voluntarily join associations and see them as satisfying both self-interests and providing public engagement? Is there a democratic ethic and mores that shape the way business is conducted and decisions are made in these associations? Do associations make citizens feel empowered to better their lives and the lives of others?

Virtues Taught by Democratic Leaders

Just as churches, families, and associations teach democratic mores, leaders also have an obligation to be advocates of the democratic idea. Part of this comes from example. The leaders of democratic regimes should be generous, wise, courageous, and just as they govern. They should be willing to go against popular sentiment if they believe it is for the public good and do all they can to inform people why they make the decisions they do. They should demonstrate moderate and frugal living themselves and encourage the same of those who have elected them. Such virtues need to be taught to the people and their connection to freedom and equality made sure. They should uphold the high virtues of their religious communities, especially those directly relevant to self-interests rightly understood. They should acknowledge the high ideals and moral accomplishments of others in the democratic regime. For a comparativist, this means that we must ask some different questions than we often do about leaders. Do leaders talk about decisions as being moral and not simply relating to self-interest? Do leaders encourage citizens to engage in civic life? Do they promote religious principles that lend support to democratic mores? Do leaders understand that democracy means more than running for office, getting elected, and passing legislation? Do leaders demonstrate noble ambition? Do they have a sense of urgency about the mores that promote freedom and equality?

Conclusion: Democracy's Delicate Balance

In this chapter little has been said about rights or government structure. This is because the greatest challenge to consolidating regimes is to nurture democratic virtues, and in established democracies, to maintain democratic virtues. Balancing rights and virtues is tricky. People must be free to do what they want but do only what is prudent. For this reason, as we study established democracies, we must do more to understand what is at the root of this delicate balance. Tocqueville reminds us that we must have free public and private associations, the teaching of particular religious principles, nurturing families, and enlightened leaders in order to maintain both equality and liberty. Too often our studies focus on problems relating to particular policies and debates without referencing these issues to the larger concerns of democracy. In doing so, we omit the essence of democracy.

A thumbnail sketch is offered of how we need to return to the idea of democracy as a regime comprised of engaged citizens, not simply a type of government. We have sacrificed much in how we focus on the few—the elites who negotiate transitions, lead the way to consolidation, and form agendas in established democracies. But we need to focus more on the idea of democracy. Why did those elites move toward democracy in the first place? What did democracy promise that motivated them? How did the idea of democracy prompt citizens in newly established democracies to consolidate gains? How does the idea of democracy keep hope alive in established democracies? It is these questions on which we need to focus. They are the questions that have fascinated political philosophers who study democracy. As comparativists, we need to renew our efforts in finding how practical experience corresponds with our philosophies of democracy. In so doing, we begin to meet the charge of Tocqueville to find a new political science so that we turn our heads from the methodological ruins of the past.

5

Conclusion

Rethinking Comparative Politics

In the late 1980s there was an explosion of scholarship on democratization. This trend continued throughout the 1990s and will no doubt continue in the years ahead. Books, articles, and papers have been written representing scholars' attempts to understand how democracy emerges in countries where authoritarianism has been the rule.[1] From these studies we have identified factors that seem to play a role in the democratization process. We have created useful frameworks that help us organize our thinking about democratic transitions and how regimes consolidate democratic gains. In studying particular governments that are under stress to liberalize, we know the kinds of things we should be looking for to offer an assessment of what is and is not going well. It is a near universal aspiration of comparativists that democracy will continue to emerge. But we are wiser now than we were several decades ago, and therefore feel less compelled to make predictions of when regimes will or will not democratize.

Recent scholarship over the last decade and a half has been helpful in terms of understanding factors that *could be* important to particular countries in the transition to and consolidation of democracy. But as nearly every study suggests, not all factors play the same role in every situation. What is helpful to democracy in one country may not be helpful at all, or may even harm, the prospects for democracy in another country. Our methods are primarily geared toward looking at features that fit particular circumstances and not necessarily features that apply to democracies in general. This is one reason why the subfield of comparative politics has once again begun emphasizing cross-national and cross-regional studies—to better understand the process of democratization wherever it occurs. These studies do not, however, study democratization across cultural, state, and geographic boundaries as much as they purport to. Instead, they teach us to look for the same kinds of things across boundaries, usually focusing on electoral institutions. For this reason, I suggest these transnational studies are not as cutting-edge as they claim to be but are instead based upon components that have played an important role in comparative studies since the 1960s and in some cases even before that.

We have decided that political parties and elections, the role of elites, legislatures, and bureaucracies should be looked at wherever we study democracy and the prospects for democracy. Scholars are in agreement that a regime must conform to certain criteria in order for it to qualify as a democracy. At the same time, these criteria must allow for cultural diversity and historical conditions that may impact the way these processes work in particular states. Hence this book shows that comparativists have decided elections are the one factor that can be used to determine the completion of a successful transition to democracy, and very often the conditions by which a regime should be considered consolidated. It has already been mentioned that this is a key reason why democracy is often defined by comparativists procedurally (free and fair elections) rather than by other means because these other means are said to relate more to preferences and particularistic cultural attributes of the persons studying democracy and not democracy itself.[2] So do we have anything approaching a grand theory of comparative politics, or do we fall short? Have we given up on a definition of democracy that speaks more to the quality of a regime and not simply democratic procedures? Are comparativists correct that the essence of democracy is really in the agency to choose elected leaders, or is there something else? Do we really understand the importance of democratic thought and the role it plays in political development, or are we merely technicians? Must we think of the problems of transition as one thing, the problems of consolidation as another thing, and the problems of established democracies as yet another thing? Is there a common connection that links problems at the various stages of democratization? If there are alternative ways of thinking about these problems, how do we go about developing them? These issues constitute the central thrust of this chapter. We begin by summarizing the strengths and weaknesses of recent studies on democracy that we considered in previous chapters. Then we look at the question of democracy as a regime. It will be argued that conceptualizing democracy differently than we do now will help us better analyze states that are not yet democracies, states that have recently become democratic, and states that have been democratic for a long time. Then a few suggestions will be offered of how we can begin to rethink our study of democratization and democratic regimes—a preliminary effort that demonstrates the need for a grand theory of comparative politics.

Comparativists' Mixed Record on Democracy

Criticism of comparative politics does not mean to imply that we have not had success in understanding the process of democratization. We have had real success. And as mentioned above, we are better able to determine what factors play a role in a country's democratic development than our scholarship allowed us prior to the third wave of democratization. But our record has been mixed. While we can identify important factors, we are not as able to assess the quality of new democracies and established democracies as well as we should be able to.

Comparativists know a great deal more about democracy now than we did forty years ago. Rustow warned us long ago about the follies of identifying criteria that "make democratic regimes" (even though he went on in the same article to set criteria of his own).[3] The third wave has produced democracies out of authoritarian regimes that we would not have expected to democratize. Income levels have not always been where we thought they should be by way of promoting economic conditions that would support democracy.[4] But democracy evolved anyway. Religious and cultural traditions have not been as resistant to democratic change as we feared they would be.[5] Once seen as immovable and ever-hateful of their democratic enemies, communist regimes sowed the seeds of their own demise, and democracy is being embraced.[6] Military regimes are not as much of an impediment to civilian rule as some feared.[7] Bureaucratic-authoritarian regimes are not as self-perpetuating as some thought them to be.[8] Authoritarian rulers proved themselves able to make the democratic changes necessary to pave a smoother transition to democracy than many thought possible.[9] We know more about the limitations of predicting democratic change based on requisites to democracy, yet we also know more about how certain factors serve as catalysts or impediments to the process of democratization in specific countries:

1. We know why certain authoritarian regimes are better than other authoritarian regimes in terms of how they treat the people. We know a little more about what characteristics of regimes are more likely to be

successful in making a peaceful transition to democracy and why certain characteristics make other regimes more likely to experience hardship that could lead to violence or failure in introducing liberal reforms.

2. We know more about why authoritarian regimes fail. We have seen that leaders may abandon authoritarianism because it is no longer considered a path that is as effective for political and economic development as it had been in the past.

3. We know that authoritarian regimes may not intend to democratize when attempting reforms but may be merely attempting to liberalize the regime. But the liberalization of a regime very often sets in motion the forces of democratization that can set a country on a path from which it is very difficult to turn away.

4. Failed attempts to democratize may only be temporary setbacks. As Huntington suggests, liberalization tends to take an inhibited course toward democracy, proceeding "two steps forward, and one step back."[10]

5. We are still struggling with the idea of elections, but most scholars are beginning to realize that elections are not a sufficient condition of democracy.[11] Elections are increasingly seen as a right belonging to a larger body of rights within any given democratic society.

6. We have a greater understanding of the role of elites. Opposition leaders who make too many short-term demands on authoritarian rulers may spoil the chances of democracy emerging. And authoritarian leaders who hold onto power at all costs without compromising with the opposition risk violence and their own overthrow or incarceration by subordinate leaders within their own regimes or by opposition leaders who gain control.[12]

7. We know that popular approval is needed to rally behind democratic changes, and that this approval needs to be directed in ways that support rule of law, even if it means that the people have to overlook the heinous acts of previous authoritarian rulers.[13]

8. We realize that in some cases it is better for economic development to follow a democratic compromise because it can lend support to the new democratic regime.[14] Citizens in newly democratized states are often willing to put off economic development for the promise of democracy.

9. We know a little more about cultural particularism, that democracy can be weakened or strengthened by the specific cultural conditions of countries. But we also recognize that particular cultural impediments to democracy are not as pronounced over time as we previously thought them to be.[15]

10. We understand circumstances a little better now than we did in regards to the timing of public policy. We have a general idea of when particular policies may work under certain conditions and when they may fail or jeopardize democratic success.[16] In particular, we are learning more about when economic policies lend support for democratic development and the sustaining of democratic gains.[17]

11. We understand more about consolidating democratic gains in general. We are rediscovering the role of social capital and the development of state and societal institutions that enhance the democratic compact in both young and established democracies.[18]

12. We are beginning to understand that minimalist definitions of democracy are simply not good enough and that democracies need to be assessed in terms of their quality and their ability to improve people's lives.[19]

13. We are better at using different kinds of tools for measurement. Comparativists are not as divided along lines of those favoring quantitative techniques against those who favor nonquantitative methods. We are better at incorporating both methods and using them in complementary ways, thus enhancing our abilities to understand democracy and democratization.[20]

14. Finally, a maturity is being reached within the subfield of comparative politics. Fewer comparativists are engaged in debates where they forward and defend extreme positions of either supporting democracies on the one hand or nondemocracies on the other. Comparative politics is not plagued with the turmoil that threatened to destroy the subfield during the 1970s and early 1980s.[21]

So with all of these successes, why do we need to rethink the direction of our scholarship? As mentioned in the first two chapters, the mixed record of comparativists can be understood by looking at the history of comparative politics as a subfield over the past fifty years or so. We started out with the noble goal of looking for reasons why leaders turned away from democracy and embraced the totalitarian philosophies of fascism and communism. Eventually many comparativists abandoned the idea of promoting democratic development and simply opted to demonstrate the shortcomings of democracy and find ways to justify nondemocratic ideologies and nondemocratic regimes. Once the third wave of democracy began, comparativists were caught largely unaware that democratization was more than simply an isolated event occurring in a handful of countries. It was, in fact, a global phenomenon. Democracy led us—we did not anticipate it—and we were therefore poorly equipped to offer much until a few pioneering studies began to emerge that served to rally comparativists and to rekindle our hopes for democracy being embraced everywhere. And while we have been fairly good at identifying the factors mentioned above, much of what comparativists have done in the past decade or so has been to reinvent the wheel. Our embracing certain methods without understanding the philosophical implications of doing so, along with our neglect of democratic philosophy in general, has left us in a position where we are duplicating much work that has already been done, particularly the work of political philosophy.

At the close of World War II, comparativists relied on the work of sociologists who had turned to ideal-type categories identified first by Max Weber and Auguste Comte.[22] The political characteristics philosophers identified with certain kinds of regimes were said to be suspect. All regimes were viewed as performing basically the same kinds of duties, the only difference being the degree of feedback policymakers agreed to listen to within the various regimes.[23] Weber's assumptions about political leadership being based upon the same principles everywhere (legal-rational, traditional, charismatic) coached us away from asking the kinds of questions political scientists had traditionally asked. They were questions first asked by the ancient Greek philosophers. How should people live their lives? What is virtue? What is justice? What is the best regime? These questions seemed corny and too bound within a particular cultural tradition for comparativists who faced the realities of a diverse and changing world.[24] Hence too many comparativists became relativist in their thinking, abandoning democracy before they ever considered the alternatives. Social science methodology determined our scholarly product before we even considered what philosophical issues were at stake. We could not defend democracy because we had not thought through what the implications for it and other kinds of regimes were. We therefore sought ways to defend our theoretical weaknesses rather than attempting to build a sound foundation that would help us understand democracy in a more complete fashion.

Our reliance on social science methodology at the expense of studying political philosophy not only left us unable to defend democracy, but also turned us into practitioners of technique rather than political scientists. Just as Weber taught that politics was a vocation, the social science methods we used convinced us that doing political science was doing the craft of a technician.[25] We have been trained in the technicalities of the field and for a time lost touch with the idea that we were supposed to identify the good and find ways to realize the good. We failed to consider human nature deeply. We failed to see that philosophical questions relating to political ideals and political goods matter. Hence we became good at showing the superficial weaknesses of a democratic system—why authoritarianism is so resilient, and how countries under specific circumstances deal with political problems—but we have had no overarching purpose or goal to our work. Even though most comparativists now accept democracy as the goal, we are relatively passionless about our work as we go about listing reasons why democracy works under some circumstances and why it doesn't work in others. We perpetuate our craft, teaching the same methods to undergraduates and graduate students who never ask the big questions of political philosophy but immediately go to work "doing their own thing," looking at this country and that country and explaining which factors work and which ones do not. We are technicians, indeed, and like the electrician who understands a circuit, but knows next to nothing about the theory of electricity, and the mechanic who understands the need to mix fuel and air in an internal combustion engine but has no idea about the physics of energy, comparativists are still too wedded to social science methodology without having an adequate understanding of the philosophy that forms the basis of their work. In this regard we have longed to follow the model of the natural sciences and to our own disadvantage we have been successful in doing so. We have found a way to describe democratization as a process that is separated from thinking about democracy. We want democracy to exist and to grow everywhere, but we are unable to explain in depth why we want democracy. We are therefore Cartesian at best. We defend democracy because it is useful to us and it satisfies our desires to live prosperous lives, but we do not justify it in the way the Greeks reminded political scientists that they should—that no question can remain unexamined and that if one regime is better than another, it must be so morally, ethically, and practically.[26]

We recognize that established democracies are experiencing a common phenomenon of mistrust toward their democratically elected leaders. We have too often fallen into the same trap as politicians of looking to simple answers to very complex questions. We consider welfare policies, education problems, crime, and matters of individual empowerment, but fail to look at the other concerns of democracy, such as civility and public virtue. We have sharpened our abilities to consider the problems of poor institutional development and the decline of social capital,[27] and while these studies touch upon some of the very issues with which Tocqueville wrestled, comparativists fail to deal with them as deeply as Tocqueville, Montesquieu, and the American founders did. This task has been left almost exclusively to political philosophers.[28]

We understand democracy by some of its parts, but we do not understand it as a whole regime. Comparativists use the term "regime" to differentiate between one kind of rule and another, but the concept of a regime is much larger. Regimes constitute ways of living, not simply types of government structures.

In sum, comparativists are ankle-deep in democratic theory when they should be immersed in it. This is not to suggest that we need to duplicate the work of political philosophy. But it does mean that comparativists should be involved in a common endeavor in writing treatises of particular nations or regions that are philosophically rich. This means we have to do a better job of assessing the quality of democracies young and old alike. In order to do this we need to think differently about what democracy means. What follows is an attempt to get us thinking more philosophically about democratization and democracy.

What Is Democracy?

In the first chapter an alternative way of thinking about democracy is offered. This definition differs from the ones comparativists typically use because it corresponds more closely to the way democracy is conceptualized by philosophers who think about democracy. It is useful here to offer a summary of that definition because it gets to the heart of where comparativists need to start thinking about democracy.

Our definition of democracy suggests we think of it as a composition of two things, rights and virtues. Rights were developed through the liberal tradition that sprang up in the Enlightenment period of the West, while republican virtues date back to the ancient Greeks. Rights are supposed to be instinctual, while virtues require education. Most comparativists have focused on rights more than virtues because rights establish real citizenship. In order for free elections to be held in a country, some acknowledgment of rights must be accepted. The problem in many countries struggling to democratize is that very often the only right initially granted is the right to vote. This can often result in elections that are democratic in the sense that people have the right to choose their leaders, but rights of speech, assembly, and dissent are withheld. When limited rights are extended, it is not a very large step backward to withdraw voting rights before or after an initial election is held. Hence even though rights are claimed to be instinctual, they are not easily won, and time is required to establish rights as a characteristic of a democratic regime. In short:

1. Rights assume human beings are free agents who are not bound by custom, ancestral tradition, or any other claims of moral and political superiority.
2. The establishment of rights gives people the freedom to challenge political authority. People have a right to scrutinize all moral, ethical, and political claims made by political leaders and fellow citizens and determine the validity of such claims. They are free to consider all matters of public policy without fear of retribution.
3. Rights give people the vote, establish free speech, freedom to assemble, and freedom to pursue their own interests in life (within the acceptable limits of a democratic society). Rights establish a basic sense of justice and equality. Rights stake a claim that democracy is the best regime and that democracy offers a greater chance for people to pursue happiness than any other form of government.

The argument presented in Chapter 4 suggests that the citizens and leaders in established democracies have perhaps become too rights-oriented. They make more demands on government and on their fellow citizens on the basis of rights, which has increased the ambivalence citizens in these countries feel toward their governments. This is also a problem of democratizing countries or countries that have established rights for the first time. Because rights give citizens the ability to challenge traditional sources of authority, ethical and moral assumptions are often challenged as well; this leaves citizens with the responsibility of choosing how to moderate their own lives in a world where self-interests can easily lead to the ruination of individuals, family, and the nation-state. For this reason virtues are needed to rein in passions that may not be checked in any other way. The puritan ideals of the early American republic (such as tolerance, civility, self-restraint, self-transcendence, frugality, courage, and moderation) helped people rely more upon sound judgment and less upon the limits of state law to check behavior that might otherwise undermine democracy. Republican virtues, therefore, should include:

1. accepted standards of right and wrong based on individual accountability and the acknowledgement that one's personal behavior has a direct influence on the well-being and happiness of others;
2. that tolerance, self-restraint, frugality, courage, and moderation bring civility and pride to public and private life in a democracy; and
3. that political leaders in democratic societies honor high moral standards and virtues.

In addition, leaders believe that their words and actions provide a moral example for others in the regime to follow.

A mature democracy emerges when a civil society is established. A civil society is the successful unity of both the liberal democracy of rights and republican democracy based on virtues.[29] Firmly grounded in ethical considerations, the individual emerges from his or her family and the institutions that have taught obedience and individual responsibility and enters into a world where law and reason rule the day.[30] Though it is a common argument that this occurs primarily within the functioning of an economic society, volunteer organizations and civic clubs play a vital role in civil society as well. Tocqueville referred to these attributes as mores, where both of the components we are discussing here lead to the situation where citizens, largely on their own, set up institutions to govern their affairs that are partially separated from or are completely distinct from the operations of government.[31] Hence the real measure of democratic success is not whether people could hold elections, or whether those holding reserve domains of power within the government decide to go along with the laws promulgated in a democratic fashion by democratically elected leaders; real democracy is measured by people's abilities to govern their affairs by themselves in a self-disciplined manner. Hence with the creation of civil society, we have the establishment of a democratic regime in its fullest.

How do we determine whether or not a state has become a full-fledged democratic regime then? Considering democracy in its parts as we have just done here allows us to determine whether a country is barely democratic or whether it is in fact on solid grounds. Has it established rights along with a generally accepted view of what is right and wrong and how citizens must act on their own to preserve the good? The proof of this would be the emergence of a dynamic and vigorous civil society. By this measurement, it is easier to determine if democracy has become, in Linz's words, "the only game in town,"—or whether there are reserve domains of power that lurk behind the scenes waiting for the chance to overturn the democratic experiment or where citizens are failing to appreciate the significance and promise of democracy for the long haul.[32] Conceptualizing democracy in this way also supports the claim made in Chapter 4 that the problems established democracies currently face differ from those developing democracies face only in scope and severity —the problems are essentially the same. All democracies wrestle with the problems of balancing rights and virtues in connection with the challenges of public policy. Established democracies struggle to elect leaders with high moral standards and keep their standards of morality steady just as developing countries do. And while we can reject arguments made against democracy or in qualifying exceptions to democracy by critics such as Singapore's Lee Kuan-Yew, Peru's Alberto Fujimori, and extremists in Russia and elsewhere, their assertions about the decadence of the West should be warnings to us to reconsider the question of civic virtues and their relation to the good life provided by democracy.

It has been argued in this book that thinking about how to define democracy is but one part of studying democratization. It has also been suggested that comparative politics has made great strides in studying democracy in the past decade or so. So how do we go from a definition of democracy to looking at how countries become democratic? How do we preserve the accomplishments of comparative politics and yet do a better job of assessing the quality of democracies?

The Process of Democratization

There are many philosophers who have demonstrated that comparing regimes requires more than looking at a single component of study. It means that we should be moving toward a grand theory of democratic development: a theory that transcends the narrowness of a single debate about whether a democratic transition is complete when a first election is held; or whether a regime is consolidated when people believe in democratic reforms; or whether there are no longer significant groups who seek to overthrow the democratic government; or whether leaders initially elected in a democratic fashion voluntarily step down when they are voted out of office in a subsequent election.[33] We need a theory that is a composition of ideas and frameworks that we currently use, based on a philosophical foundation that analyzes human nature, understands democracy as a regime, and allows us to assess states in transition to democracy and states that are already democratic. We need a theory that helps us look beyond the single self-interests of leaders making democratic compromise and encourages us to consider other motives. We need a framework that helps us determine if leaders have a concept of what the best regime is, and whether policy proposals to realize the best are too ambitious or not ambitious enough, and whether they contain the seeds of liberalism. In established democracies a grand theory would help us determine if regimes have strayed from the democratic standard and whether politicians and scholars are asking the right kinds of questions about these regimes.

In Chapter 1 it is suggested that Aristotle and Montesquieu have already provided examples of what comparative studies ought to aspire to. Both philosophers offer sophisticated analyses of human nature and what this means for regime development. They demonstrate that human beings have a potential to do both good and evil. For this reason, they justify why some regimes will make people better, and others will bring out the worst in people.

Aristotle shows how reason and virtue can guide human beings. He argues that human beings are more likely to fulfill their potential to do good in a democratic (or in his words, a mixed) regime than any other regime. He tells us that we need to study the parts of the regime.[34] Who makes up the regime? To what do the citizens of a regime aspire? To what is it that their leaders aspire? Is there a middle class that moderates the tension between the other classes in the regime? What role do and should education and culture play in the regime? In some respects one might ask, how does this differ from some of our comparative studies, especially those attempting to study a regime by the methodology set out by Almond and Verba in *The Civic Culture*? Almond himself, after all, asserts that the idea of a civic culture can be traced to Aristotle and other Greek philosophers.[35] The answer lies in the assumptions made in both studies. Almond and Verba suggest that the primary determinant in the process of democratization or in maintaining democracy is attitudinal. Great effort is made in the civic culture literature to employ various methods for gathering and analyzing data in order to determine what people are or are not thinking about, and whether or not this conforms to the expectations we have of a democratic regime.[36] Aristotle also believed there are attitudinal factors at play in a mixed regime along with many other important considerations as well. He wanted us not only to look at the commonality of democratic regimes, but in considering a regime's parts, to ask another question: What has a regime determined as the highest goal to which human beings can aspire, and is this goal attainable? He did not want to simply look at what a regime is or is not doing to become democratic, he wanted to prescribe a remedy to cure regimes of the ills that keep them from becoming better. He was not content with minimal definitions of democracy that have to conform to a wide range of social science theorizing about societies in general, but was concerned about the development of a democratic regime in the fullest. His critique of modern comparative studies might include praise for scholarship that understands the "political moments" of democratic compromise, understanding political culture, and the role of elites, but criticism that the essence of democracy is lost by a failure to see *democracy as a regime that encompasses more than simply the sphere of government and political struggle.* Democratic regimes are constantly facing change. Regimes contain elements that are both democratic and non-democratic. Aristotle taught us that states do not simply acquire ideological justifications for democracy. There are certain principles that leaders and citizens must consider and embrace if democracy is to be shored up.

In a similar fashion, Montesquieu gave us an enormously important comparison of authoritarian, monarchical, and democratic regimes in his *Spirit of the Laws.*[37] He analyzed human nature and the importance of discovering rights before one can justify democracy. He demonstrated how virtues support these rights and how an imbalance in either leads to democracy's demise. Within these parameters, Montesquieu considered political leadership, the role of religion, the role of culture, the importance of economic systems, and how the various forms of education, formal and informal, sustain the different kinds of regimes. His work is a careful reminder that the constitution of a democratic state is not a document promulgated by people's representatives in a constitutional congress. A democratic regime is constituted by its complex parts and interplay of rights, virtues, and institutions that are both inside and outside the formal boundaries of established government. Thinking of democracy in this way keeps us from the pitfalls of relying on a single explanation for justifying democratic success or failure. High income alone, for example, does not account for democratic stability as some recent scholarship suggests.[38] Montesquieu agreed with the importance of a prosperous society but also pointed to the need for frugality and moderation—virtues that are upheld in a regime that contains a variety of income-earning groups. Liberal philosophy teaches us that decision-making moments where authoritarianism is abandoned and democracy is upheld are more than breakthroughs. They are acknowledgments of rational thinking and faith in the promise of democratic regimes to deliver in ways authoritarianism cannot.

Frances Fukuyama has been widely criticized for his assertion that democracy was the good that human beings were seeking and that this search was close to being realized everywhere.[39] In some respects this criticism is warranted given the fact that at least one-half of the world remains under authoritarian rule. In other respects, however, Fukuyama's assertion is testimony to the power of what democracy has demonstrated all over the world and has led to its widespread acceptance. In his preface to *Democracy in America*, Tocqueville made a bold proclamation that captures this promise of democracy. As the spirit of democracy spreads, people

> can imagine a society in which all men, regarding the law as their common work, would love it and submit to it without difficulty; the authority of the government would be respected as necessary, not as sacred; the love felt toward the head of state would be not a passion but a calm and rational feeling. Each man having some rights and being sure of the enjoyment of those rights, there would be established between all classes a manly confidence and a sort of reciprocal courtesy, as far removed from pride as from servility.
>
> Understanding its own interests, the people would appreciate that in order to enjoy the benefits of society one must shoulder its obligations. Free association of the citizens could then take the place of individual authority from the nobles, and the state would be protected both from tyranny and from license.[40]

This image of democratic transition is not widely accepted by contemporary theorists. Comparativists complain that explanations like Tocqueville's description of cultural change is unnecessarily biased and relies on a linear view of democratic development.[41] In some regards, as mentioned in Chapter 2, such criticisms are warranted. But in other respects Tocqueville's critics overlook the realities of democratic development. Though not making an argument on behalf of democracy, Hegel described the close correlation between certain ideas and the development of a modern nation-state in his *Introduction to the Philosophy of History*.[42] He argued that the philosophical and religious foundations of a society had a great deal to do with how people and leaders viewed democracy and the modern state. If philosophy, art, literature, and science enjoy some independence from religious influences and traditional cultures, Hegel demonstrated that these states embraced liberal theories more readily, whereas traditional societies found numerous religious and philosophical objections to extending freedoms to people. Hence there was no development of a civil society in traditional states because the ideas necessary to break people free had not yet been discovered in these regions of the world.

We are careful nowadays not to make such bold assertions for fear of offending those who object to the spread of philosophical ideas that originated in the West. Yet attempts to establish a notion of rights based on non-Western religious traditions and philosophies have proven unsuccessful. Those who work with such international organizations as the UN and the Red Cross have increasingly turned away from alternative notions of political rights because they are philosophically indefensible and therefore ultimately unenforceable by domestic or international law.[43] Nongovernmental human rights organizations are increasingly abandoning particularistic cultural arguments for establishing human rights because leaders of authoritarian states are finding it difficult to defend human rights abuses in the face of international conventions they depend upon for economic support and security.[44] Indeed, scholars are becoming increasingly convinced that there are no distinctive values that belong to Asia, Latin America, Africa, or Europe that cannot be changed with a serious study of political philosophy and regime choice. Doing so liberates human beings from the shackles of traditional authority that prevents human beings from discovering rights. Hegel saw that this was already happening in the West and believed this quest for understanding freedom began with political philosophy. He believed Western philosophers provided the path that others would follow. This is not to suggest that human rights are particularly Western. They are common to all peoples everywhere and therefore need the same kind of scrutiny whether we study China, Venezuela, or Portugal. Because human rights are claimed to be universal, democracy must be claimed to be universal in some fashion as well. For democracy is the only real defense of human rights because it establishes the contract within which rights thrive. Because of demonstration effects, rights language has become universal. We use democratic jargon in international meetings and organizations where democratic and nondemocratic states are represented. Nondemocratic states commonly refer to rights, even though these rights are not protected by law and even though those things claimed as rights may not be rights at all. But all of this speaks to the validity of Tocqueville's assertion that democracy would sweep the globe.

This is important for the establishment of human rights, democracy, and for our study of democratic development in general. Just as some scholars claim that democracy emerges as a result of conflict and compromise that leads to "political moments"—crucial junctures where a democratic deal is finally hammered out—democratic philosophy reminds us that in accepting such a view, we tend to overlook the other important influences that lead to compromise. Some suggest that democratic ideals and notions of rights and virtues emerge during the consolidation phase of democracy.[45] Some suggest that countries are having an easier go with it if they can complete a transition and then develop economically later.[46] Hence they reject the idea that democratic ideals can be embraced in the way Tocqueville suggested. To them it is an all elite-dependent process. But we need to ask basic questions: What goals are reformers trying to fulfill? What alternatives are acceptable? What claims are authoritarians making? Can these claims be taken seriously? What is the thinking behind the calls for reform? Some scholars make it sound as though changing regimes is as straightforward as changing shoes. Where a change is made in favor of democracy, there is more than self-interest involved. The success of these ideas in general has proven Jefferson's assertion in the Declaration of Independence to be valid, that these truths are indeed self-evident.

Yet we are resistant to considering democratization in this way because comparativists have convinced themselves that it misses the critical features of democracy. Democratization, they say, is brought about by the few, on a trial-and-error basis. This process eventually exhausts all other regime choices but democracy. If these claims are correct, however, why is it that conflict and compromise within regimes, and attempts to democratize and follow up with economic reforms, very seldom resulted in democratic success thirty years ago? What is different now from earlier times? Is it that authoritarians are exhausted in their efforts to withstand the democratic onslaught? And if this is the case, what is different about their exhaustion now compared with their willingness to resist democracy earlier?[47] Perhaps all of this suggests that the idea of necessary preconditions to democracy is not as far fetched as we thought. We should not create checklists and schemes that qualify regimes as democratic, but we should acknowledge liberalism's growing acceptance, be it economic, political, or social, because it leads to democratic compromise. We are willing to admit that authoritarians are hesitant to be the last of their species. Does this suggest democracy evolves by exhaustion, or is this an acknowledgement that democracy is in fact a better regime than other kinds of regimes? Is it necessary for every country to pass through every precondition or attribute of democracy, or is it more like Tocqueville suggests, that the spirit of democracy is almost like a "divine decree" that has mandated democracy by "providence?"[48] Is it not true that more and more countries are doing what Hegel argued they would do, that people everywhere are discovering challenges to traditional authority and justifying their lives on the basis of personal drives for freedom?[49] We see justifications for all of these assertions in the valiant attempts people have made to become democratic. Russians are disappointed that their economic woes persist in spite of the fact that they have experimented (in large measure unsuccessfully) with democracy. The wealth and political security of the West provided enough of an influence on Russians that they peacefully abandoned one of the harshest regimes known to humankind in order to acquire democracy for themselves. The people of Spain and Portugal put off economic reforms, not because they are unimportant to democratic success, but because they felt some surety that prosperity would come in time within a democratic society. Mongolians have neither next-door neighbors who are democratic nor economic wealth. They have no tradition of a continuous struggle for democracy nor outside pressure to democratize. And yet Mongolia has developed democratic institutions that are stable and promising. Many worried that the division of Czechoslovakia into the Czech Republic and Slovakia would result in war and possibly destabilize a number of countries in the region. But the careful guidance of democratic leaders and democratic experience moderated attitudes and assisted in the peaceful separation of both states.

Rather than offering a short list of things that comparativists need to do in studying democracy, some principles that point to our need to develop a grand theory for studying democracy are summarized:

1. Comparativists must ground their work in political philosophy, showing linkages of human nature and human beings' potential to do good. We can suggest how people should live their lives and see how this compares to what regimes are doing in practice.

2. We need to accept a sophisticated definition of democracy that is based upon an understanding of rights and complemented by virtues. We need to accept that a democratic regime means more than a form of government and a set of procedures; it is in fact a way of living.

3. We need a theory that helps us scrutinize how traditions, cultures, religions, and leaders stand in relation to our democratic ideal.

4. We need a theory that helps us look at how convincing the idea of democracy is compared to the principles that uphold other regimes. This will help us understand how the groundwork is prepared for conflict and compromise that lead to democracy. It also gives us a barometer to consider issues being debated in established democracies.

5. We need to consider the problems of democratizing countries and established democracies as essentially the same. We need to consider that politics is more than simply who gets what and more than an elaboration of what people expect. Comparativists need to determine whether people's expectations are realistic and suggest what kinds of things a polity should be debating.

6. We must consider how democracy is taught in the countries we study. We need to look at formal institutions, schools, and religions and determine whether or not the principles of democracy are accepted and what kinds of civic duties and virtues are taught that will have political significance for regime development. We also need to look at the ways children are taught at home and educated by government leaders because so much of our ethical outlook on life is fostered within the family and by leaders who provide standards for us to follow.

A Brief Conclusion

This chapter is not an attempt to give a full-fledged theory of how comparativists should study democracy, but instead a preliminary sketch of how we might begin building a grand theory of comparative politics —one that will help us assess the quality of democracy in both democratizing and established democratic regimes. Much of this work must begin in how we study and teach democracy in the subfield of comparative politics.

The premise of this book has been that comparativists have made real progress in studying democratization but not as much as if we had a better grounding in democratic philosophy. It has been demonstrated that the subfield of comparative politics abandoned liberal philosophy in favor of some useful, though often poorly thought-out, social science methods; that in the last decade or so, we have rediscovered the promise and hope of democracy, though our studies are still rather superficially developed because we have neglected political thought. As a result, we teach what we know to undergraduates and graduate students and give them a mistaken view of comparative politics, one that is in large part technique and only in small measure founded on theory.

This is not to suggest that studies that look at specific aspects of democratization, or that quantitative studies that measure public attitudes or analyses of specific policies, are unimportant. The point is that these studies are not only useful, but can help us learn even more if we are able to anchor our work upon the foundation where all subfields of political science should be anchored. That foundation is political philosophy. By not doing this, we run a risk of doing what we did in the 1970s—dividing along ideological and methodological lines, undermining our ability to champion democracy.

Philippe Schmitter and Terry Lynn Karl argued in an early issue of the *Journal of Democracy* that democracy had been treated by comparativists and policymakers as a devalued currency.[50] They attempted to redeem democracy by providing a definition of democracy that was comprehensive and yet allowed for some variation. This book has suggested that we need a definition of democracy that is not a hard currency but a gold standard, one that provides an ideal to measure democratic regimes in their various stages of development. This requires us to look at the first questions political philosophers consider. Then our definition will have grounding, and we will know better what we are looking for when we study democracy.

Notes

Notes to Chapter 1

1. Vaclav Havel, "Politics and Conscience," p. 267.
2. "In Mexico, a New Era and . . . a New Deal?" *New York Times*, July 4, 2000, p. A7.
3. Fareed Zacharia, "Culture Is Destiny," pp. 221–23.
4. Francis Fukuyama, *The End of History and the Last Man*, p. xii.
5. Hannah Arendt, *The Origins of Totalitarianism*.
6. John L. Esposito and John O.Voll, *Islam and Democracy*.
7. Adrian Karatnycky, *Freedom in the World*, p. 5.
8. Fareed Zakaria, "The Rise of Illiberal Democracy," pp. 242–58.
9. Karl J. Fields, *Enterprise and the State in South Korea and Taiwan*.
10. Monsignor Vincent A. Yzermas, *American Participation in the Second Vatican Council*, pp. 618–27.
11. Second Vatican Council, "Declaration on Religious Freedom," pp. 350–53.
12. Farhat Haq, "Jihad over Human Rights," p. 245.
13. Ann Elizabeth Mayer, *Islam and Human Rights*, pp. 16–17.
14. Gabriel A. Almond, *A Discipline Divided*, pp. 36–37.
15. Aristotle, *Politics*, pp. 94–95.
16. Charles de Secondat Montesquieu, *Spirit of the Laws*, Part I, Books 2 and 3.
17. Max Weber, *From Max Weber*.
18. David Easton, *A Framework for Political Analysis*.
19. Gabriel A. Almond and Sidney Verba, *The Civic Culture*.
20. Lucian Pye and Sidney Verba, *Political Culture and Political Development*, p. 11.
21. Ibid., pp. 544–50.
22. Peter B. Evans, Dietrich Rueschemeyer, and Theda Skocpol, *Bringing the State Back In*.
23. Guillermo O'Donnell, *Modernization and Bureaucratic-Authoritarianism*.
24. Fernando Henrique Cardoso and Enzo Faletto, *Dependency and Development in Latin America*.
25. Ronald H. Chilcote, *Theories of Comparative Politics*, p. 251.
26. Samuel P. Huntington, *Political Order in Changing Societies*.
27. Juan J. Linz and Alfred Stepan, *The Breakdown of Democratic Regimes*.
28. Leonard Binder, et al., *Crises and Sequences in Political Development*.
29. Samuel P. Huntington, *The Third Wave*. Huntington argues the first wave of

155

democracy (1828–1926) was closely associated with the American and French revolutions, the second wave (1943–1962) the aftermath of World War II, and the third wave (beginning in 1974) following the liberalization of communist and noncommunist authoritarian regimes.

30. Two of the most influential of these studies are Guillermo O'Donnell and Philippe C. Schmitter, *Transitions from Authoritarian Rule*, and Larry Diamond, Juan Linz, and Seymour Martin Lipset, *Politics in Developing Countries*.

31. Joseph A. Schumpeter, *Capitalism, Socialism, and Democracy*; Robert A. Dahl, *Polyarchy*.

32. Schumpeter, *Capitalism, Socialism, and Democracy*, p. 269.

33. Dahl, *Polyarchy*, p. 1.

34. Ibid., p. 2.

35. Ibid., p. 8.

36. Ibid., p. 14.

37. Philippe C. Schmitter and Terry Lynn Karl, "What Democracy Is . . . and Is Not," pp. 75–89.

38. Aristotle's *Politics*, Plato's *Republic*, and the Socrates' *Apology*, are only a few of the major works that consider the dangers of democracy.

39. John Locke, *Two Treatises of Government*.

40. Thomas Jefferson, Declaration of Independence.

41. James Madison, "Federalist 51."

42. James Madison, "Federalist 10."

43. Montesquieu, *The Spirit of the Laws*, Books 3, 4, 8, 24.

44. Thomas Jefferson, "Letter to Thomas Law."

45. William A. Galston, *Liberal Purposes*; Thomas Pangle, *The Ennobling of Democracy*, p. 107.

46. Tocqueville, *Democracy in America*, Book II, Part 1, chaps. 2 and 5, and Part 3.

47. G.W.F. Hegel, *Hegel's Philosophy of Right*, pp. 266–67.

48. Robert D. Putnam, *Bowling Alone*.

49. O'Donnell and Schmitter, *Transitions from Authoritarian Rule*. p. 6.

50. Richard Gunther, Nikiforos P. Diamandouros, and Hans-Jurgen Puhle, eds., *The Politics of Democratic Consolidation*, p. 3.

51. Juan J. Linz and Alfred Stepan, *Problems of Democratic Transition and Consolidation*, p. 3.

52. Andreas Schedler, "What Is Democratic Consolidation?" pp. 91–107.

53. Adam Przeworski, et al., "What Makes Democracies Endure?" pp. 39–55.

54. Guillermo O'Donnell, "Transitions, Continuities, and Paradoxes," p. 18.

55. Schedler, "What Is Democratic Consolidation?" pp. 100–101.

56. Linz and Stepan, *Problems of Democratic Transition and Consolidation*, p. 6.

Notes to Chapter 2

1. Immanuel Kant, *Perpetual Peace*.

2. Schmitter and Karl, "What Democracy Is . . . and Is Not."

3. Max Weber, *The Protestant Ethic and the Spirit of Capitalism*.

4. Gabriel A. Almond, *A Discipline Divided*, pp. 13–29.

5. Daniel Lerner, *The Passing of Traditional Society*.

6. W.W. Rostow, *The Stages of Economic Growth*, chap. 2.

7. Seymour Martin Lipset, *Political Man*, p. 31.

8. Andre Gunder Frank, "Sociology of Development and Underdevelopment," pp. 20–73.

9. Pye and Verba, *Political Culture and Political Development*, pp. 11–13.

10. Terry Lynn Karl, "Dilemmas of Democratization in Latin America."

11. David Easton, *The Political System*; and *A Framework for Political Analysis*.

12. Almond and Verba, *The Civic Culture*, pp. 11–12.

13. Ibid., p. 13.

14. Ibid., pp. 29–30.

15. Ibid., p. 30.

16. Carole Pateman, "The Civic Culture," p. 59.

17. Arend Lijphart, "The Comparable Cases Strategy in Comparative Research."

18. Pye and Verba, *Political Culture and Political Development*, chap. 1.

19. Pateman, "Philosophic Critique," pp. 97–98.

20. Almond, *A Discipline Divided*, pp. 23–4. See also Chilcote, *Theories of Comparative Politics*, pp. 36–40.

21. Huntington, *Political Order in Changing Societies*.

22. Ibid., p. 5.

23. Ibid., pp. 8–9.

24. Dankwart A. Rustow, "Transitions to Democracy," 1970.

25. Leonard Binder, et al., *Crises and Sequences in Political Development*.

26. Ibid., pp. 302–303.

27. Andre Gunder Frank, "The Development of Underdevelopment," pp. 17–31.

28. Guillermo A. O'Donnell, *Modernization and Bureaucratic-Authoritarianism*.

29. Cardoso and Faletto, *Dependency and Development in Latin America*, pp. 175–76.

30. Chilcote, *Theories of Comparative Politics*, chaps. 5 and 9.

31. Howard J. Wiarda, "The Ethnocentrism of the Social Science Implications of Research and Policy," pp. 163–96.

32. Edmund Husserl, *Phenomenology and the Crisis of Philosophy*, pp. 80–99.

33. Chilcote, *Theories of Comparative Politics*, p. 421; Wiarda, "The Ethnocentrism of Social Science."

34. See *Journal of Democracy* (April 2001), series of articles entitled "High Anxiety in the Andes."

35. Fernando Henrique Cardoso, "Democracy as a Starting Point," pp. 8–9.

36. See Aristotle's *Politics*, Montesquieu's *Spirit of the Laws*, and *The Federalist Papers*.

37. O'Donnell and Schmitter, *Transitions from Authoritarian Rule*, p. 19.

38. Huntington, *The Third Wave*, pp. 44–46.

39. Linz and Stepan, *Problems of Democratic Transition and Consolidation*, p. 49.

40. Nancy Bermeo, "Rethinking Regime Change," p. 376.

41. O'Donnell and Schmitter, *Transitions from Authoritarian Rule*, p. 52.

42. Kim Dae Jung, "Is Culture Destiny? The Myth of Asia's Anti-Democratic Values."

43. Francis Fukuyama, "The Illusion of Exceptionalism."

44. Mayer, *Islam and Human Rights*, pp. 52–3.

45. Linz and Stepan, *Problems of Democratic Transition and Consolidation*, p. 74.

46. Ibid., p. 71.

47. O'Donnell and Schmitter, *Transitions from Authoritarian Rule*, p. 34.

48. Linz and Stepan, *Problems of Democratic Transition and Consolidation*, pp. 66–67.

49. Some scholars refer to this process as political learning. See Nancy Bermeo, "Democracy and the Lessons of Dictatorship," pp. 273–76.

50. Steven J. Hood, *The Kuomintang and the Democratization of Taiwan*; Karl J. Fields, *Enterprise and the State in Korea and Taiwan*.

51. Andreas Schedler, "Mexico's Victory."

52. Linz and Stepan, *Problems of Democratic Transition and Consolidation*.

53. Phillipe C. Schmitter, "Dangers and Dilemmas of Democracy," p. 59.

54. Dorothy Solinger, "Ending One-Party Dominance."

55. Ibid., p. 32.

56. Huntington, *The Third Wave*, pp. 266–67.

57. Juan J. Linz and Alfred Stepan, eds., *The Breakdown of Democratic Regimes: Part I; Crisis, Breakdown, and Reequilibration*.

58. O'Donnell and Schmitter, *Transition from Authoritarian Rule*, p. 29.

59. Ronald Inglehart, *Modernization and Postmodernization*, pp. 329–30.

Notes to Chapter 3

1. Steven Levitsky, "Fujimori and Post-Party Politics in Peru," p. 81.

2. Peru's first political party, the Alianza Popular Revolucionaria, continues to have a large following today.

3. Philip Mauceri, *State Under Siege*, pp. 149–55.

4. John Crabtree, *Peru Under Garcia*.

5. Ernesto Garcia Calderon, "High Anxiety in the Andes," pp. 46–48.

6. Maxwell A. Cameron, "Self-Coups," p. 126.

7. Levitsky, "Fujimori and Post-Party Politics in Peru," p. 80.

8. United States Department of State, "Background Note."

9. United States Department of State, Bureau of Democracy, Human Rights, and Labor. "Peru Country Report on Human Rights Practices for 1997."

10. These are all problems that faced Fujimori early in his administration, though he has failed to address them effectively. See Peter Hakim and Abraham F. Lowenthal, "Latin America's Fragile Democracies," pp. 16–29. For factual and statistical information relating to social indicators, see the chapter on Peru in *Europa Yearbook*.

11. Calderon, "High Anxiety in the Andes," p. 57.

12. *Free China Journal*, April 15, 1994.

13. Hood, *The Kuomintang and the Democratization of Taiwan*, p. 163.

14. Ibid., chaps. 7 and 8.

15. Schumpeter, *Capitalism, Socialism, and Democracy*, pp. 290–96.

16. Lipset, *Political Man*, pp. 12–13, 38.

17. Almond and Verba, *The Civic Culture*, pp. 29–31.

18. Dahl, *Polyarchy*, p. 8.

19. Linz and Stepan, *The Breakdown of Democratic Regimes*.

20. Larry Diamond, "Is the Third Wave Over?"

21. Adam Prezworski, Adam Michael Alvarez, Jose A. Cheibub, and Fernando Cimonji, "What Makes Democracies Endure?" pp. 31–56.

22. Guillermo O'Donnell, "Illusions About Consolidation," pp. 37–47.

23. Guillermo O'Donnell, "Democratic Theory and Comparative Politics."

24. Andreas Schedler, "What Is Democratic Consolidation?" pp. 91–107.

25. See the discussion by Linz and Stepan in *Problems of Democratic Transition and Consolidation* for a discussion of the weakness of this argument.

26. Gunther, Diamandouros, and Puhle, *The Politics of Democratic Consolidation*, pp. 12–13.

27. Larry Diamond, "Rethinking Civil Society," pp. 6–11.

28. Linz and Stepan, *Problems of Democratic Transition and Consolidation*, p. 10.

29. Karl, "Dilemmas of Democratization in Latin America," pp. 5–6.

30. Inglehart, *Modernization and Postmodernization*, p. 5.

31. Gunther, Diamandouros, and Puhle, *The Politics of Democratic Consolidation*, pp. 393–94.

32. Francis Fukuyama and Sanjay Marwah, "Comparing East Asia and Latin America."

33. Information gathered from group discussions with faculty members of the University of Lima, Lima, Peru, October 14–27, 2001.

34. In a recent work, Ronald Inglehart has indicated that cultures are also deeply impacted by political ideas that shape the behaviors of societies as well. See his "Culture and Democracy."

35. Guillermo O'Donnell, "Transitions, Continuities, and Paradoxes," p. 20.

36. Linz and Stepan, *Problems of Democratic Transition and Consolidation*, p. 6.

37. Ibid., p. 14, 35.

38. Juan J. Linz, Alfred Stepan, and Richard Gunther, "Democratic Transition and Consolidation in Southern Europe with Reflections on Latin America and Eastern Europe," pp. 83–84.

39. Gunther, Diamandouros, and Puhle, *The Politics of Democratic Consolidation*, p. xiii.

40. Ibid., pp. 19–20.

41. Linz and Stepan, *Problems of Democratic Transition and Consolidation*, p. 457.

42. Felipe Aguero, "Democratic Consolidation and the Military in Southern Europe and South America," p. 165.

43. Huntington, *The Third Wave*, pp. 259, 270.

44. Linz and Valenzuela, *The Failure of Presidential Democracy*, pp. 73–87.

45. Gunther, Diamandouros, and Puhle, *The Politics of Democratic Consolidation*, p. 396, 402.

46. Huntington, *The Third Wave*, p. 272.

47. Linz and Stepan, *Problems of Transition and Consolidation*, p. 139.

48. Ibid., pp. 113–14.

49. Linz and Stepan, *Problems of Transition and Consolidation*, p. 435.

50. Juan J. Linz and Arturo Valenzuela, *The Failure of Presidential Democracy*.

51. Linz, Stepan, and Gunther, "Democratic Transition and Consolidation in South America," p. 122.

52. Linz and Stepan, *Problems of Democratic Transition and Consolidation*, p. 83.

53. Huntington, *The Third Wave*, pp. 273–74.

54. United States Department of State, "Background Notes."

55. Adrian Karatnycky, "A Good Year for Freedom," p. 7.

56. Robert Putnam's work has been especially important in this regard. See his books *Making Democracy Work* and *Bowling Alone*, and "Democracy in the World."

Notes to Chapter 4

1. Montesquieu, *Spirit of the Laws*, Part II, Book 9, chap. 1, p. 131.

2. Aristotle, *Politics*, Book 7, chap. 4; David Hume, "Idea of a Perfect Commonwealth," pp. 527–28.

3. Madison, "Federalist 10."

4. See Susan J. Pharr and Robert D. Putnam, eds., *Disaffected Democracies*.

5. Putnam, *Making Democracy Work*; Francis Fukuyama, *Trust*.

6. Michael W. Foley and Bob Edwards, "The Paradox of Civil Society."

7. Among these are Bellah's *Habits of the Heart*, Putnam's *Making Democracy Work*, and his *Bowling Alone* and "Democracy in the World." There are scores of other articles and books by both comparativists and political philosophers on Tocqueville as well.

8. There are several good editions of *Democracy in America*. The edition I refer to in this book and in the notes for this chapter is translated by George Lawrence and edited by J.P. Mayer.

9. Book I, Part 2, chap. 9, p. 287.

10. Tocqueville's "Introduction," p. 9.

11. Book I, Part 2, chap. 4.

12. Book I, Part 2, chap. 6.

13. Book I, Part 2, chap. 6, p. 245.

14. Book I, Part 2, chap. 9, p. 292.

15. Tocqueville's "Introduction," p. 16.

16. Book I, Part 2, chap. 9, pp. 292, 299–300.

17. Book I, Part 1, chap. 2, p. 47.

18. Ibid., p. 47.

19. Ibid., p. 292.

20. Book I, Part 2, chap. 9, pp. 288, 291.

21. Ibid., p. 294, and Book II, Part 1, chap. 5, p. 444.

22. Book I, Part 1, chap. 2, pp. 36–45.

23. Ibid., pp. 44–45.

24. Book II, Part 2, chap. 17, p. 547.

25. Book II, Part 1, chap. 5, p. 443.

26. Book II, Part 2, chap. 1, pp. 505–506.

27. Book I, Part 2, chap. 9, p. 297.

28. Book II, Part 2, chap. 15, p. 545.

29. Book II, Part 1, chap. 5, p. 449.

30. Book I, Part 2, chap. 9, p. 303.

31. Ibid., p. 291.

32. Ibid.

33. Book I, Part 2, chap. 4, pp. 192–93.
34. Book II, Part 2, chap. 5, pp. 516–17.
35. Ibid., p. 515.
36. Book II, Part 2, chap. 7, pp. 522–23.
37. Book II, Part 2, chap. 5, p. 511.
38. Book I, Part 1, chap. 2, p. 47, and Book II, Part 3, chap. 17, p. 615.
39. Book II, Part 3, chap. 19, pp. 627–30.
40. Tocqueville's "Introduction," p. 17.
41. Book II, Part 3, chap. 17, p. 615.
42. Book II, Part 3, chap. 1, pp. 561–65, and Book II, Part 3, chap. 2.
43. Book II, Part 2, chap. 8, p. 525.
44. Ibid., p. 526.
45. Book II, Part 2, chap. 15, p. 542.
46. Book II, Part 2, chap. 8, p. 527.
47. Book II, Part 2, chap. 2, pp. 506–508.
48. Book II, Part 2, chap. 4, p. 509.
49. Book I, Part 2, chap. 5, p. 225.
50. Tocqueville's "Introduction," p. 13.
51. Book I, Part 2, chap. 9, p. 302.
52. Book I, Part 2, chap. 5, p. 206.
53. Tocqueville's "Introduction," pp. 12–13.
54. Pippa Norris, ed., *Critical Citizens*, pp. 269–70.
55. Robert D. Putnam, *Making Democracy Work.*
56. Putnam, "Bowling Alone," pp. 73–76. See also his book *Bowling Alone.*
57. Michael W. Foley and Bob Edwards, "Is It Time to Disinvest in Social Capital?"
58. Sheri Berman, "Civil Society and the Collapse of the Weimar Republic," pp. 401–429. See also Berman's "Civil Society and Political Institutionalization," pp. 562–574.
59. Putnam, *Bowling Alone*, p. 409.
60. Samuel Huntington, "Will More Countries Become Democratic?" pp. 189–201.
61. Enrique Krauze, "Mores and Democracy in Latin America," pp. 20–21.
62. Esposito and Voll, *Islam and Democracy.*
63. Aristotle, *Politics*, Book 3, chap. 4.

Notes to Chapter 5

1. Alfred Stepan, *Arguing Comparative Politics.* Another useful, though dated, summary of these studies has been done by Shin Doh Chull, "On the Third Wave of Democratization."
2. Guillermo O'Donnell, "Horizontal Accountability in New Democracies," pp. 112–126.
3. Rustow, "Transitions to Democracy," pp. 337–63.
4. Lipset, *Political Man*, chap. 2.
5. Huntington, "Will More Countries Become Democratic?" pp. 188–207.
6. John T. Ishimaya, "Communist Parties in Transition," pp. 147–66.
7. Something Huntington pointed out earlier in *Political Order in Changing Societies.*

8. O'Donnell, *Modernization and Bureaucratic-Authoritarianism*.

9. Bermeo, "Rethinking Regime Change," pp. 359–377.

10. Huntington, *The Third Wave*, chap. 5.

11. Even O'Donnell is trying to refine his position taken earlier on this matter. See his "Democratic Theory and Comparative Politics."

12. O'Donnell and Schmitter, *Transitions from Authoritarian Rule*.

13. Huntington, *The Third Wave*, pp. 213–14.

14. Linz and Stepan, *Problems of Transition and Consolidation*, p. 139.

15. Inglehart, *Modernization and Postmodernization*, p. 5.

16. Linz and Stepan, *Problems of Transition and Consolidation*, p. 435; see also Karl's "Dilemmas of Democratization in Latin America."

17. Prezworski, et al., "What Makes Democracies Endure?" pp. 39–55.

18. Putnam, *Making Democracy Work*.

19. Elshtain, *Democracy on Trial*, chap. 5.

20. Inglehart, *Modernization and Postmodernization*.

21. Almond, *A Discipline Divided*; see also Chilcote, *Theories of Comparative Politics*, chap. 1; and Howard J. Wiarda, *New Directions in Comparative Politics*, pp. 3–30.

22. Max Weber, *The Methodology of the Social Sciences*; Stanislav Andreski, ed., *The Essential Comte*.

23. David Easton, *The Political System*.

24. Pye and Verba, *Political Culture and Political Development*.

25. Max Weber, "Politics as a Vocation," in H.H. Geurth and C. Wright Mills, eds., *From Max Weber's Essays in Sociology*.

26. Rene Descartes, "Some Moral Rules Derived from the Method," in *Discourse on Method*, pp. 15–19. By contrast see "Pericles' Funeral Oration," in Thucydides, *Complete Writings*.

27. Fukuyama, *Trust*; and Putnam, *Making Democracy Work*.

28. Sanford Kessler, *Tocqueville's Civic Religion*; and Pangle, *Ennobling of Democracy*.

29. Hegel, *Philosophy of Right*, pp. 122–55. See also Steven B. Smith, *Hegel's Critique of Liberalism*, p. 128, and pp. 140–44.

30. Paul Franco, *Hegel's Philosophy of Freedom*, pp. 236–55.

31. Tocqueville, *Democracy in America*, Book 2, Part 1, chaps. 2 and 5, and Part 3.

32. Huntington, "Democracy for the Long Haul," pp. 3–13.

33. See chaps. 2 and 3 to review the scholarship on these debates.

34. Aristotle, *Politics*. See also Mary P. Nichols, *Citizens and Statesmen*, pp. 90–100.

35. Almond and Verba, *The Civic Culture Revisited*, chap. 1.

36. Almond and Verba reject this criticism of the civic culture study, but it is a criticism that is well grounded and held by many scholars. See their defense of the civic culture study in the introductory chapter of *Civic Culture Revisited*.

37. Montesquieu, *Spirit of the Laws*.

38. Przeworski, et al., "What Makes Democracies Endure?" pp. 39–55.

39. Fukuyama, *The End of History and the Last Man*.

40. Tocqueville, *Democracy in America*, p. 14.

41. Rustow, "Transitions to Democracy," pp. 337–363.

42. Hegel, *Introduction to the Philosophy of History*.

43. See Joanne Bauer and Daniel Bell, eds., *The East Asian Challenge for Human Rights*. See also Nicholas O. Berry, *War and the Red Cross*.

44. Amartya Sen, "Democracy as a Universal Value," pp. 3–17; Andrew J. Nathan, Linda Bell, and Ilan Peleg, eds., *Negotiating Culture*.

45. Karl, "Dilemmas of Democratization in Latin America."

46. Linz and Stepan, *Problems of Transition and Consolidation*, p. 139.

47. Consuelo Cruz, "Identity and Persuasion," pp. 275–312.

48. Tocqueville, *Democracy in America*, Book. 1, p. 7.

49. O'Donnell, "Democratic Theory and Comparative Politics," pp. 17–18.

50. Schmitter and Karl, "What Democracy Is . . . and Is Not," pp. 75–89.

Bibliography

Aguero, Felipe. 1995. "Democratic Consolidation and the Military in Southern Europe and South America." In *The Politics of Democratic Consolidation: Southern Europe in Comparative Perspective*, ed. Richard Gunther, Nikiforos P. Diamandouros, and Hans Jurgen Puhle. Baltimore, MD: Johns Hopkins University Press.

Almond, Gabriel A. 1990. *A Discipline Divided: Schools and Sects in Political Science*. Newbury Park, CA: Sage.

Almond, Gabriel A., and Sidney Verba. 1963. *The Civic Culture: Political Attitudes and Democracy in Five Nations*. Princeton, NJ: Princeton University Press.

———, eds. 1980. *The Civic Culture Revisited*. Boston: Little, Brown.

Andreski, Stanislav, ed. 1974. *The Essential Comte*. New York: Barnes and Noble.

Arendt, Hannah. 1966. *The Origins of Totalitarianism*. New York: Harcourt, Brace and World.

Aristotle. 1984. *Politics*. Ed. Carnes Lord. Chicago: University of Chicago Press.

Bauer, Joanne, and Daniel Bell, eds. 1999. *The East Asian Challenge for Human Rights*. Cambridge: Cambridge University Press.

Bellah, Robert N. 1986. *Habits of the Heart: Individualism and Commitment in American Life*. New York: Harper and Row.

Berman, Sheri. 1997. "Civil Society and the Collapse of the Weimar Republic." *World Politics* 49 (April 1): 401–429.

———. 1997. "Civil Society and Political Institutionalization." *American Behavioral Scientist* 40 (March/April): 561–574.

Bermeo, Nancy. 1990. "Rethinking Regime Change." *Comparative Politics* 22 (April): 359–377.

———. 1992. "Democracy and the Lessons of Dictatorship." *Comparative Politics* 24 (April): 273–291.

Berry, Nicholas O. 1997. *War and the Red Cross: The Unspoken Mission*. New York: St. Martin's.

Binder, Leonard, et al. 1971. *Crises and Sequences in Political Development*. Princeton, NJ: Princeton University Press.

Bloom, Allan, ed. 1968. *The Republic of Plato*. New York: Basic Books.

Calderon, Ernesto Garcia. 2001. "High Anxiety in the Andes: Peru's Decade of Living Dangerously." *Journal of Democracy* 12 (April): 46–58.

Cameron, Maxwell A. 1998. "Self-Coups: Peru, Guatemala, and Russia." *Journal of Democracy* 9 (January): 125–139.

Cardoso, Fernando Henrique. 2001. "Democracy as a Starting Point." *Journal of Democracy* 12 (January): 5–14.

Cardoso, Fernando Henrique, and Enzo Faletto. 1979. *Dependency and Development in Latin America.* Trans. Marjory Mattingly Uriquidi. Berkeley: University of California Press.

Chilcote, Ronald H. 1981. *Theories of Comparative Politics: The Search for a Paradigm.* Boulder, CO: Westview Press.

Crabtree, John. 1992. *Peru Under Garcia: An Opportunity Lost.* Pittsburgh, PA: University of Pittsburgh Press.

Cruz, Consuelo. 2000. "Identity and Persuasion: How Nations Remember Their Pasts and Make Their Futures." *World Politics* 52 (April): 275–312.

Dahl, Robert A. 1971. *Polyarchy: Participation and Opposition.* New Haven, CT: Yale University Press.

Declaration of Independence. 1776.

Descartes, Rene. 1956. *Discourse on Method.* Upper Saddle River, NJ: Prentice-Hall/Library of Liberal Arts.

Diamond, Larry. 1994. "Rethinking Civil Society: Toward Democratic Consolidation." *Journal of Democracy* 5 (July): 1–15.

———. 1996. "Is the Third Wave Over?" *Journal of Democracy* 7 (July): 20–37.

Diamond, Larry, Juan Linz, and Seymour Martin Lipset, eds. 1990. *Politics in Developing Countries.* Boulder, CO: Lynne Rienner.

Easton, David. 1953. *The Political System: An Inquiry into the State of Political Science.* New York: Alfred A. Knopf.

———1965. *A Framework for Political Analysis.* Englewood Cliffs, NJ: Prentice-Hall.

Elshtain, Jean Bethke. 1995. *Democracy on Trial.* New York: Basic Books.

Esposito, John L., and John Voll. 1996. *Islam and Democracy.* New York: Oxford University Press.

Evans, Peter B., Dietrich Rueschemeyer, and Theda Skocpol, eds. 1985. *Bringing the State Back In.* Cambridge: Cambridge University Press.

Fields, Karl J. 1995. *Enterprise and the State in South Korea and Taiwan.* Ithaca, NY: Cornell University Press.

Foley, Michael W., and Bob Edwards. 1996. "The Paradox of Civil Society." *Journal of Democracy* 7 (July): 38–52.

———. 1999. "Is It Time to Disinvest in Social Capital?" *Journal of Public Policy* 19 (April): 141–173.

Franco, Paul. 1999. *Hegel's Philosophy of Freedom.* New Haven, CT: Yale University Press.

Frank, Andre Gunder. 1966. "The Development of Underdevelopment." *Monthly Review* (September): 17–31.

———. 1967. "Sociology of Development and Underdevelopment." *Catalyst* 3 (Summer): 20–73.

Fukuyama, Francis, and Sanjay Marwah. 2000. "Comparing East Asia and Latin America: Dimensions of Development." *Journal of Democracy* 11 (October): 80–94.

Fukuyama, Francis. 1992. *The End of History and the Last Man.* New York: Free Press.

———. 1995. *Trust: The Social Virtues and the Creation of Prosperity.* New York: Free Press.

———. 1997. "The Illusion of Exceptionalism," *Journal of Democracy* 8 (October): 80–94.

Galston, William A. 1991. *Liberal Purposes: Goods, Virtues, and Diversity in the Liberal State.* Cambridge: Cambridge University Press.

Gerth, H.H., and C. Wright Mills, eds. 1946. *From Max Weber: Essays in Sociology.* New York: Oxford University Press.

Gunther, Richard, Nikiforos P. Diamandouros, and Hans Jurgen Puhle, eds. 1995. *The Politics of Democratic Consolidation: Southern Europe in Comparative Perspective.* Baltimore, MD: Johns Hopkins University Press.

Hakim, Peter, and Abraham F. Lowenthal. 1991. "Latin America's Fragile Democracies." *Journal of Democracy* 2 (Summer): 16–29.

Haq, Farhat. 2001. "Jihad over Human Rights: Clash of Universals." In *Negotiating Culture and Human Rights*, ed. Lynda S. Bell, Andrew J. Nathan, and Ilan Peleg. New York: Columbia University Press.

Havel, Vaclav. 1991. *Open Letters: Selected Writings, 1965–1990.* New York: Alfred A. Knopf.

Hegel, G.W.F. 1952. *Philosophy of Rights.* Trans. T.M. Knox. London: Oxford University Press.

———. 1988. *Introduction to the Philosophy of History.* Trans. Leo Rauch. Indianapolis, IN: Hackett.

Hood, Steven J. 1997. *The Kuomintang and the Democratization of Taiwan.* Boulder, CO: Westview Press.

Hume, David. 1987. *Essays: Moral, Political, and Literary.* Ed. Eugene F. Miller. Indianapolis: Liberty Classics.

Huntington, Samuel P. 1968. *Political Order in Changing Societies.* New Haven, CT: Yale University Press.

———. 1984. "Will More Countries Become Democratic?" *Political Science Quarterly* 99 (Summer): 189–201.

———. 1991. *The Third Wave: Democratization in the Late Twentieth Century.* Norman: University of Oklahoma Press.

———. 1996. "Democracy for the Long Haul." *Journal of Democracy* 7 (April): 3–13.

Huntington, Samuel P., and Lawrence E. Harrison. 2000. *Culture Matters: How Values Shape Human Progress.* New York: Basic Books.

Husserl, Edmund. 1965. *Phenomenology and the Crisis of Philosophy: Philosophy as a Rigorous Science, and Philosophy and the Crisis of European Man.* Trans. Quentin Lauer. New York: Harper and Row.

Inglehart, Ronald. 1997. *Modernization and Postmodernization: Cultural, Economic, and Political Change in 43 Societies.* Princeton, NJ: Princeton University Press.

——— 2000. "Culture and Democracy." In *Culture Matters: How Values Shape Human Progress*, ed. Lawrence E. Harrison and Samuel P. Huntington. New York: Basic Books.

Ishimaya, John T. 1995. "Communist Parties in Transition: Structures, Leaders, and Processes of Democratization in Eastern Europe." *Comparative Politics* 27 (January): 147–166.

Jefferson, Thomas. 1975. "Letter to Thomas Law, June 13, 1814," In *The Portable Thomas Jefferson.* Ed. Merrill D. Peterson. New York: Viking-Penguin.

Kant, Immanuel. 1970. *Kant's Political Writings.* Ed. Hans Reiss. Cambridge: Cambridge University Press.

———. 1970. "Perpetual Peace: A Philosophical Sketch." In *Kant's Political Writings.* Ed. Hans Reiss. New York: Cambridge University Press.

Karatnycky, Adrian. 2000. *Freedom in the World: The Annual Survey, 1998–1999.* New York: Freedom House.

Karl, Terry Lynn. 1990. "Dilemmas of Democratization in Latin America." *Comparative Politics* 23 (October): 1–21.

Kessler, Sanford. 1994. *Tocqueville's Civic Religion: American Christianity and the Prospects for Freedom*. Albany, NY: State University of New York Press.

Kim Dae Jung. 1994. "Is Culture Destiny? The Myth of Asia's Anti-Democratic Values." *Foreign Affairs* 73 (November/December): 189–194.

Krauze, Enrique. 2000. "Mores and Democracy in Latin America." *Journal of Democracy* 11 (January): 18–24.

Lerner, Daniel. 1958. *The Passing of Traditional Society: Modernizing the Middle East*. Glencoe, IL: Free Press.

Levitsky, Steven. 1999. "Fujimori and Post-Party Politics in Peru." *Journal of Democracy* 10 (July) 78–92.

Lijphart, Arend. 1975. "The Comparable Cases Strategy in Comparative Research." *Comparative Political Studies* 8 (July): 158–177.

Linz, Juan, and Alfred Stepan, eds. 1978. *The Breakdown of Democratic Regimes*. Baltimore, MD: Johns Hopkins University Press.

———. 1996. *Problems of Democratic Transition and Consolidation: Southern Europe, South America, and Post-Communist Europe*. Baltimore, MD: Johns Hopkins University Press.

Linz, Juan J., Alfred Stepan, and Richard Gunther. 1995. "Democratic Transition and Consolidation in Southern Europe with Reflections on Latin America and Eastern Europe." In *The Politics of Democratic Consolidation: Southern Europe in Comparative Perspective*, ed. Gunther, Diamandouros, and Puhle. Baltimore, MD: Johns Hopkins University Press.

Linz, Juan J., and Arturo Valenzuela. 1994. *The Failure of Presidential Democracy: Comparative Perspectives*. Baltimore, MD: Johns Hopkins University Press.

Lipset, Seymour Martin. 1981. *Political Man: The Social Bases of Politics*. Baltimore, MD: Johns Hopkins University Press.

Locke, John. 1988. *Two Treatises of Government*. Ed. Peter Laslett. New York: Cambridge University Press.

Madison, James. 1961. "Federalist 10" and "Federalist 51." In *The Federalist Papers*. Ed. Clinton Rossiter. New York: NAL Penguin.

Maher, Joanne, ed. 2003. *The Europa World Yearbook*, Volume II. London: Europa Publications Ltd.

Mauceri, Philip. 1996. *State Under Seige: Development and Policy Making in Peru*. Boulder, CO: Westview Press.

Mayer, Ann Elizabeth. 1999. *Islam and Human Rights: Tradition and Politics*. Boulder, CO: Westview Press.

Montesquieu, Charles de Secondat. 1989. *Spirit of the Laws*. Trans. Anne M. Cohler, Basia C. Miller, and Harold Stone. New York: Cambridge University Press.

Nathan, Andrew J., Linda Bell, and Ilan Peleg, eds. 2000. *Negotiating Culture: Implications of the Human Rights Debate for Universalism and Relativism*. New York: Columbia University Press.

Nichols, Mary P. 1992. *Citizens and Statesmen: A Study of Aristotle's Politics*. Savage, MD: Rowman and Littlefield.

Norris, Pippa, ed. 1999. *Critical Citizens: Global Support for Democratic Governance*. Oxford: Oxford University Press.

O'Donnell, Guillermo. 1973. *Modernization and Bureaucratic-Authoritarianism: Studies in South American Politics*. Berkeley, CA: University of California, Institute of International Studies.

———. 1986. "Transitions, Continuities, and Paradoxes." In *Transitions from Authoritarian Rule*, ed. Guillermo O'Donnell and Philippe Schmitter. Baltimore: Johns Hopkins University Press.

———. 1996. "Illusions About Consolidation." *Journal of Democracy* 7 (April): 34–51.

———. 1998. "Horizontal Accountability in New Democracies." *Journal of Democracy* 9 (July): 112–126.

———. 1999. "Democratic Theory and Comparative Politics." Paper presented at the annual meeting of the American Political Science Association, Atlanta, August 26–29, 1999.

O'Donnell, Guillermo, and Philippe C. Schmitter. 1986. *Transitions from Authoritarian Rule*. Baltimore, MD: Johns Hopkins University Press.

———. 1993. *Transitions from Authoritarian Rule: Tentative Conclusions About Uncertain Democracies*. Baltimore, MD: Johns Hopkins University Press.

Pangle, Thomas A. 1992. *The Ennobling of Democracy: The Challenge of the Postmodern Age*. Baltimore, MD: Johns Hopkins University Press.

Parsons, Talcott. 1951. *The Social System*. Glencoe, IL: Free Press.

Pateman, Carole. 1980. "The Civic Culture: A Philosophic Critique." In *The Civic Culture Revisited*, ed. Gabriel A. Almond and Sidney Verba. Newbury Park, CA: Sage.

Peterson, Merrill D., ed. 1975. *The Portable Jefferson*. New York: Penguin.

Pharr, Susan J., and Robert D. Putnam, eds. 2000. *Disaffected Democracies: What's Troubling the Trilateral Countries?* Princeton, NJ: Princeton University Press.

Plato. 1984. "Socrates' Apology." In *Four Texts on Socrates, Revised Edition*, ed. Thomas G. West and Grace Starry West. Ithaca, NY: Cornell University Press.

Plattner, Marc F., and Larry J. Diamond, eds. 2000. "Democracy in the World: Tocqueville Reconsidered," *Journal of Democracy* 11, no. 1 (January).

Przeworski, Adam, Michael Alvarez, Jose A. Cheibub, and Fernando Cimonji. 1996. "What Makes Democracies Endure?" *Journal of Democracy* 7 (January): 39–55.

Putnam, Robert D. 1993. *Making Democracy Work: Civic Traditions in Modern Italy*. Princeton, NJ: Princeton University Press.

———.1995. "Bowling Alone: America's Declining Social Capital." *Journal of Democracy* 6 (January): 65–78.

———. 2000. *Bowling Alone: The Collapse and Revival of American Community*. New York: Simon and Schuster.

Pye, Lucian W., and Sidney Verba, eds. 1965. *Political Culture and Political Development*. Princeton, NJ: Princeton University Press.

Rossiter, Clinton, ed. 1961. *The Federalist Papers*. New York: Penguin.

Rostow, W.W. 1962. *The Stages of Economic Growth: A Non-Communist Manifesto*. Cambridge: Cambridge University Press.

Rustow, Dankwart A. 1970. "Transitions to Democracy: Toward a Dynamic Model." *Comparative Politics* 2 (April): 337–363.

Rynne, Xavier. 1966. *The Fourth Session: The Debates and Decrees of Vatican Council II, September 14 to December 8, 1965*. New York: Farrar, Straus, and Giroux.

Schedler, Andreas 1998. "What Is Democratic Consolidation?" *Journal of Democracy* 9 (April): 91–107.

———. 2000. "Mexico's Victory: The Democratic Revolution." *Journal of Democracy* 11 (October): 5–19.

Schmitter, Philippe C. 1994. "Dangers and Dilemmas of Democracy." *Journal of Democracy* 5 (April): 57–74.

Schmitter, Philippe C., and Terry Lynn Karl. 1991. "What Democracy Is. . . and Is Not." *Journal of Democracy* 2 (Summer): 75–89.

Schumpeter, Joseph A. 1942. *Capitalism, Socialism, and Democracy.* New York: Harper and Row.

Second Vatican Council. 1965. "Declaration of Religious Freedom," December 7, 1965. In Xavier Rynne, *The Fourth Session: The Debates and Decrees of Vatican Council II, September 14 to December 8, 1965.* New York: Farrar, Straus, and Giroux.

Sen, Amartya. 1999. "Democracy as a Universal Value." *Journal of Democracy* 10 (July): 3–17.

Shin Doh Chull. 1994. "On the Third Wave of Democratizaton." *World Politics* 47 (October): 135–170.

Smith, Steven B. 1989. *Hegel's Critique of Liberalism: Rights in Context.* Chicago: University of Chicago Press.

Solinger, Dorothy. 2001. "Ending One-Party Dominance: Korea, Taiwan, Mexico." *Journal of Democracy* 12 (January): 30–42.

Stepan, Alfred. 2001. *Arguing Comparative Politics.* New York: Oxford University Press.

Thucydides. 1951. "Pericles' Funeral Oration." In *Complete Writings: The Peloponnesian War.* Trans. John H. Finley, Jr. New York: Modern Library.

de Tocqueville, Alexis. 1969. *Democracy in America.* Trans. George Lawrence, ed. J.P. Mayer. New York: Harper and Row.

U.S. Department of State. 2001. "Background Note: Peru." Washington, DC: Government Printing Office.

U.S. Department of State, Bureau of Democracy, Human Rights, and Labor. 1998. "Peru: Country Report on Human Rights Practices for 1997." Washington, DC: Government Printing Office.

Weber, Max. 1949. *The Methodology of the Social Sciences.* Trans. and ed. Edward A. Shils and Henry A. Finch. New York: Free Press.

———. 1958. *From Max Weber: Essays in Sociology.* Trans. and ed. H.H. Gerth and C. Wright Mills. New York: Oxford University Press.

———. 1958. *The Protestant Ethic and the Spirit of Capitalism.* Trans. Talcott Parsons. New York: Charles Scribner's Sons.

Wiarda, Howard J. 1981. "The Ethnocentrism of Social Science: Implications of Research and Policy." *The Review of Politics* 43 (April): 163–197.

———. 1991. *New Directions in Comparative Politics.* Boulder, CO: Westview Press.

Yzermas, Monsignor Vincent A., ed. 1967. *American Participation in the Second Vatican Council.* New York: Sheed and Ward.

Zacharia, Fareed. 1994. "Culture Is Destiny: A Conversation with Lee Kuan Yew." *Foreign Affairs* 73 (March/April): 325–351.

——— ed. 1999. "The Rise of Illiberal Democracy." In *The New Shape of World Politics*, ed. Fareed Zacharia. New York: W.W. Norton.

Index

171

Steven J. Hood is Professor of Politics at Ursinus College. He has written extensively on East Asian politics, issues of democratization, and debates concerning universal democratic values.